Advance Praise for
It's Not the Size of the Data— It's How You Use It

"A fascinating combination of rigorous research and methodology with practical insights and implications. Both practitioners and academics can benefit from reading it."
—Don Lehmann, George E. Warren Professor of Business, Columbia University; coauthor of *Analysis for Marketing Planning, Managing Customers as Investments, Product Management*, and others

"Big data in marketing is about looking for rationality to emotional behavior. This book teaches how to do that."
—Stan van den Broek, Shopper Insights Manager, SCA Hygiene Products

"Pauwels uses numerous examples to present scientific knowledge in an impressively simple and understandable way. An extremely informative book that will inspire many managers to make immediate changes in handling their data."
—David Geistert, Department of Business Administration— Market-Oriented Media, University of Hamburg

"Way more than just metrics and dashboards—this will be a great resource for marketers and business professionals."
—Laura Patterson, author of *Marketing Metrics in Action* and *Measure What Matters*, and cofounder of VisionEdge Marketing, Inc.

It's Not the Size of the Data

It's How You Use It

Smarter Marketing with Analytics and Dashboards

Koen Pauwels

AMACOM AMERICAN MANAGEMENT ASSOCIATION

NEW YORK · ATLANTA · BRUSSELS · CHICAGO · MEXICO CITY
SAN FRANCISCO · SHANGHAI · TOKYO · TORONTO · WASHINGTON, D.C.

Bulk discounts available. For details visit:
www.amacombooks.org/go/specialsales
Or contact special sales:
Phone: 800-250-5308
Email: specialsls@amanet.org
View all the AMACOM titles at: www.amacombooks.org
American Management Association: www.amanet.org

This publication is designed to provide accurate and authoritative information in regard to the subject matter covered. It is sold with the understanding that the publisher is not engaged in rendering legal, accounting, or other professional service. If legal advice or other expert assistance is required, the services of a competent professional person should be sought.

Library of Congress Cataloging-in-Publication Data
Pauwels, Koen
  It's not the size of the data—it's how you use it : smarter marketing with analytics and dashboards / Koen Pauwels.
      pages cm
  Includes bibliographical references and index.
  ISBN-13: 978-0-8144-3395-9
  ISBN-10: 0-8144-3395-2
  1. Marketing research. 2. Marketing research—Data processing. 3. Dashboards (Management information systems). I. Title.
  HF5415.2.P39 2014
  658.8'302855437—dc23

2013031903

About AMA
American Management Association (www.amanet.org) is a world leader in talent development, advancing the skills of individuals to drive business success. Our mission is to support the goals of individuals and organizations through a complete range of products and services, including classroom and virtual seminars, webcasts, webinars, podcasts, conferences, corporate and government solutions, business books and research. AMA's approach to improving performance combines experiential learning—learning through doing—with opportunities for ongoing professional growth at every step of one's career journey.

Printing number
10 9 8 7 6 5 4 3 2 1

For the best support in decisions and in life:
to my family first of
Leopold, Rosa, Gerben, and Herman
and to my family forward of
Zeynep, Kerem, and Mir

Contents

Foreword

REGIS MCKENNA is attributed with saying that marketing represents the ongoing effort to keep products and services in touch with evolving conditions. As the pace of change has accelerated, so have the degree of choices and point of control—choice of product, choice of brand, choice of channels, and choice of touch points. The customer, as they say, is firmly in the driver's seat. As a result, marketers and marketing have evolved from selling products and building relationships to creating compelling customer experiences. This in turn has led to a proliferation of content, and a focus on segmentation, customization, personalization, and engagement.

This multichannel, customer-driven dynamic environment presents increasing challenges. There are more claims on your customers, your company, and your attention, time, and energy. Every day more opportunities present themselves to marketing, such as new online communities, new channels of communication, and new markets and customer segments. So how do you decide where to make your investments? It's often a tough choice—one that can be made easier if you have the right insights from the right information, organized in the right way. That's why the principles in this book are applicable to every marketer everywhere.

I first met Dr. Koen Pauwels in 2007 when we were both attending a marketing conference. It wasn't long before we recognized that we were kindred spirits in our dedication to enabling organizations to use data, analytics, process, and metrics to improve marketing alignment and accountability. Since then, we have continued to help each other's efforts and those of marketers who want to operate centers of excellence.

I believe every marketing professional is committed to generating value. But let's face it; every marketing investment is under intense scrutiny. The need for a good rationale to invest the resources you have available was never more of a prerequisite than it is today. One of the quotes in this book I encourage we all commit to memory is "Gut decisions, which were once seen as inspired (if they succeeded), are now viewed as rash. To command authority, you need the numbers to back you up." That's why I encourage you to move this book to the top of your pile.

The basic idea behind this book seems rather obvious. By using data, analytics, modeling, data visualization, and dashboards, marketers can make better strategic and tactical decisions and investments. If only it were that simple. Koen Pauwels is clear right out of the gate—it may not be simple but it is essential. The Advertising Research Foundation's fortieth annual conference in 2001 was among the first to boldly address the topic of marketing measurement and accountability. And it's likely to remain a top-of-mind topic—a topic that has remained among the headlines ever since marketers started scrambling to crack the code, some more successfully than others. But all of us are exposed. What we can measure, the data we can collect, has exploded as quickly as the channels and technologies we have at our fingertips.

What Koen Pauwels has brought into focus is that, at a time when we have more marketing data and technology than ever before, we must undertake an immense effort to transition from activity-based to outcome-based marketing. This transformation involves embracing the science, and thus the difficult and what may at first glance seem like the dry side of marketing.

How can marketing prove and improve its value? That's the question that has driven VisionEdge Marketing since its inception. We know from our work in hundreds of engagements that marketers who create alignment, leverage data and analytics, identify and select the right metrics, and employ an effective dashboard are more successful, more confident, and more credible. This is the beauty in science side of marketing.

Through this book Koen Pauwels makes his extensive experience within the reach of us all. He outlines steps, shares case studies, and provides end-of-chapter guidelines that make it possible for marketers to create and utilize dashboards as a way to both monitor progress and facilitate decisions. He designed this book to help marketers use data and metrics to better understand the effect and impact of marketing investments.

For any marketer who wants to generate value, enable his or her company to compete successfully, and prove its value, read on. If you want to avoid swimming aimlessly in a sea of data and metrics, then this book is for you. If you want to better understand how to select metrics and present data, then start by turning the page.

Laura Patterson
author of *Marketing Metrics in Action: Creating a Performance-Driven Marketing Organization* and *Measure What Matters: Reconnecting Marketing to Business Goals* and cofounder of VisionEdge Marketing, Inc.

Acknowledgments

AMONG THE MANY WONDERFUL PEOPLE that helped me throughout my professional development, I especially want to thank my advisor Dominique Hanssens, who continues to be an inspiration and a mentor. Likewise, I thank my academic colleagues at the Tuck School of Business and at Ozyegin University for their support. The scientific evidence for this book's insights comes from studies with several co-authors, including Shuba Srinivasan, Martin Lautman, Gokhan Yildirim, Marc Yanhuele, Amit Joshi, Evert de Haan, Jorge Silva-Risso, Sunil Gupta, Thorsten Wiesel, and Pavel Kireyev. Laura Patterson and Guy Powell both inspired me by their books on marketing performance management. Laura wrote the foreword to this book, and Guy Powell was so kind to give most useful and detailed comments. My colleagues at Marketing Productivity Group, including Craig Stacey, Stephen Dubuque, and Todd Kirk, provided contacts and empirical data for many of the U.S. case studies in this book. European and Asian case studies appear thanks to colleagues Joep Arts (Oxyme), Joris Merks (Google), Alfred Dijs, and Bernadette van Ewijk (AIMark). The ideas in this book were discussed and refined with dozens of managers, including the participants in the (executive) MBA programs at Tuck and Ozyegin University, and the annual Marketing Performance seminars of the GfK Academy in Mainz and of HEC Geneva. Especially important, Olena Svatko did a fantastic job drafting sections of this book, and motivating me throughout the process.

Decisions That Data and Analytics Can Inform

Gut decisions, which were once seen as inspired (if they succeeded), are now viewed as rash. To command authority, you need the numbers to back you up. —ANINDYA GHOSE, 2013

I know that I ought to be looking at big data, but I am not quite sure why, how, and what decisions I would be making differently as a result. —ANONYMOUS DESPERATE MANAGER, 2013

MARKETING IS AT A CROSSROADS. Managers are frustrated by the gap between the promise and the practice of effect measurement, between big data and online/offline integration. Caught between financial accountability and creative flexibility, most chief marketing officers don't last long in their companies. Their bosses have woken up to the fact their companies make million-dollar decisions based on less data and analytics than they devote to thousand-dollar operational changes. Customer and market data management, product innovation and launch, international budget allocation, online search optimization, and the integration of social and traditional media are just some of the profitable growth drivers that greatly benefit from analytical insights and data-driven action.

Such data-driven action typically involves the following four questions[1]:

1. What happened?
2. Why did it happen?
3. What will happen if?
4. What should happen?

Better, faster, and more transparent answers to these questions help establish marketing accountability.

Yet marketing accountability—let alone the accurate calculation of return on marketing investment (ROMI)—remains an elusive goal for most companies, which are struggling to integrate big and small data and marketing analytics into their marketing decisions and operations. In their March 2013 article, McKinsey experts share that "in our experience, the missing step for most companies is spending the time required to create a simple plan for how data, analytics, frontline tools, and people come together to create business value. The power of a plan is that it provides a common language allowing senior executives, technology professionals, data scientists, and managers to discuss where the greatest returns will come from and, more important, to select the two or three places to get started."[2]

The benefits of "getting started" and "marketing smarter" are huge in both academic studies and business cases. Even a small improvement in using marketing analytic dashboards brings companies on average 8 percent higher return on assets compared to their peers.[3] This benefit increases to 21 percent for firms in highly competitive industries. Organizations of any size and in any industry have seen sustainable competitive advantage from using marketing analytic dashboards. However, only 16 percent of large international companies use marketing analytics.[4] In my experience, this percentage is even lower for small and medium-sized firms across America, Europe, and Asia. I see similar issues across multinationals and companies with a few dozen employees and in industries ranging from business-to-consumer, government, and business-to-business. The next three short stories illustrate the issues that have inspired this book.

In early 2012, I found myself at the U.S. headquarters of a fast-moving consumer goods multinational. I had been called in to moderate the discussion between the chief financial officer (CFO) and the chief marketing officer (CMO) on marketing effectiveness. The CFO insisted on measuring all main activities either by ROMI or by return on marketing objective (ROMO). The list of activities included market research, marketing data management, offline marketing communications, online marketing communications, promotions, and direct marketing. Across all activities, the CFO was unhappy and had three concerns: objectives were not clearly defined, the timing of expected returns was not specified, and the marketing department showed resistance to measurement. I helped the CMO to:

- ► Clarify marketing objectives and align them with the business strategy.
- ► Overcome marketing's resistance to measurement.
- ► Obtain excellent and relevant data.
- ► Develop the analytics that showed not just the size but also the timing of the profit returns to marketing investment in all categories.

The second illustrative tale took place in an executive meeting at a European-based business-to-business manufacturer. Country managers were accustomed to obtaining a certain percentage of their revenues to spend on marketing. Faced with new competitive threats, all decision makers felt that this rule was far from optimal and needed to change—but how? Some countries asked for more money for joint promotions with their customers—to then sell more of their product to end consumers. Others considered this simply giving away money to the customers, and instead advocated a direct-to-consumer campaign to create awareness and preference for their product. Still a third group believed the firm should target policy makers directly with sustainable business credentials, pointing to huge successes of having a prime minister come talk at the company's trade shows. Unfortunately, the lack of before/after measurement of sales lift left country managers unwilling the change their positions. In this case, I worked in three steps. First, I ensured that each campaign had a stated, measurable objective that was defined in place and time and had a before/after measurement as backup. Second, after collecting data across years and countries, I categorized all campaigns by objective and ran analytical modeling to quantify the link between each objective and profits, accounting for country differences. Third, I recommended an improved allocation in the direction of the findings.

The third story I want to share involves an Asian manufacturer of consumer durables who had only sixty employees and nobody in charge of data maintenance, let alone of the analytics to make them actionable. Managers were overwhelmed by the hundreds of online metrics regarding their paid, earned, and owned media, and had little insight in the exact costs or returns of their offline marketing, which makes up 85 percent of their budget. When sales quotas loomed, they would often "shoot from the hip"—doubling spending on marketing actions that were untargeted and probably inefficient. A nagging feeling was telling them they might be increasing sales, but at the expense of profits. Moreover, several customers told them they put in an offline order based on online marketing touch points. Should online be credited for offline sales? The offline marketing manager definitely did not think so! I worked with both the offline and the online marketing manager to discuss how both channels contributed to sales. Based on this framework, the company put in place the right metrics and collected the data over time. A marketing analytics dashboard allowed both managers to play around with spending scenarios and observe the projected size and timing of profits, not just sales. They agreed on dramatic budget shifts and saw their company's profit—and their reputations—greatly increase!

Across these cases, we see the same three issues:

1. Unclear vision on how objectives relate to company performance.

2. Uncertainty on the size and timing of expected returns to marketing investment.

3. Resistance to measurement.

Sound familiar? Wouldn't it be great to have a comprehensive set of steps that can help you improve marketing decisions at your company? How about a book that is steeped in both scientific research and practical applications to guide you along?

This book is all about marketing analytics dashboards, what they are, how you can develop, use, and renovate them—and how they help you make better decisions. This book guides you along a full journey of data, analytics, dashboard insights, and the action they inspire. In specific chapters, you will learn the dashboard lingo, how to start the dashboard initiative, how to build it, design it, and implement it, and how to renovate the dashboard to maintain its relevance to decision makers in your organization. This book doesn't shy away from the tough parts, both technically and practically, and it gives special attention to hot topics such as leveraging online data and emerging markets. You will learn about what worked to overcome obstacles, how specific companies did it, and what the evidence shows for your situation.

Welcome to the brave new world of marketing analytics dashboards.

PART ONE

What Marketing Analytics Dashboards Can Do for You

CHAPTER 1

Marketing Analytics Dashboards: What, Why, Who, and How

Data is prolific but usually poorly digested, often irrelevant and some issues entirely lack the illumination of measurement.

—JOHN D.C. LITTLE,[1] 1970

LITTLE'S QUOTE RINGS AS TRUE TODAY as it did more than forty years ago, reflecting the tension between the abundance of marketing data at our disposal and the lack of actionable insights that derive from it. The advent of the Internet and recent availability of "big data" have only increased the need to distill relevant information from a wealth of data. Don't get me wrong: I love big data, but, as with other things in life, it's not about size, but what you do with it. Managers I've worked with across industries and countries know that more data does not mean more insights for action. While many feel overwhelmed by big data, others feel they don't have enough of the right data to connect each marketing action to profit outcome. For example, a bricks-and-clicks client contrasted the wealth of information provided by Google Analytics with its inability to match direct mail lists with sales or to attribute a purchase to a specific marketing action (see the case study "The Right Chair #1" later in this chapter). They wanted a marketing analytics dashboard that connected online and offline marketing, metrics, and profits, and allowed the decision makers to run easy what-if scenarios. Feeling comfortable with comparing different plans, they ran a field experiment proving a fourteen-fold increase in profit—as promised by the analytics behind the dashboard.

Wouldn't it be great if you could drive your company like a car or a plane? Thousands of bits and pieces of potentially important information feed into the few metrics that show up on your vehicle dashboard. You don't need to know everything that is under the hood to drive the vehicle!

In the last decade, the implementation of data analytics and dashboards has generated and saved millions of dollars at hundreds of firms, some of which I was fortunate to work with.[2] Firms are using dashboards to track marketing effectiveness and guide decision making in industries as disparate as business communication (Avaya), online services (Google), financial services (Ameritrade, Morgan Stanley), systems integration (Unisys), technology and electronics (SAP, Lenovo), fast-moving consumer goods (Heineken), and manufacturing (Timken).

SAP and Vanguard provide excellent video case studies on the benefits of dashboards—and the currently unfulfilled opportunities they present. Their dashboards measure outcomes important to each business, intermediate funnel metrics, their marketing campaigns, and other activities that drive them. The SAP video[3] shows how an individual decision maker uses the dashboard, while the Harvard video case on Vanguard[4] shows how the dashboard is used in group decision making, in this case an executive meeting. As a result, marketing has moved from an expense to an investment with measurable returns.

Still, most current dashboards fail to leverage data analytics to provide the needed insights for action. Vanguard CMO Sean Hagerty acknowledges: "What is missing is the connection between the individual activities and those outcomes. The next question is: how do you link the long-term measures to the short-term measures? So do awareness and image attributes translate to sales? And I don't know how to answer the question. That I think is the Holy Grail. We have not really solved that."[5] Indeed, many managers continue to be disappointed with their ability to connect marketing actions to key performance indicators and ultimately to the financial outcomes (sales, profits, stock market capitalization) that matter to the company and pay the bonuses of C-level executives. The current frustration or fatigue rests with "reporting dashboards." Reporting dashboards simply track metrics without showing which matters most to performance, and they don't permit the user to shift marketing budgets around and compare the predicted outcome in what-if analyses. Enter "marketing analytics," which provides the backbone of the visually attractive dashboard face.

Marketing analytics translates rich data into actionable insights and what-if analyses to test different scenarios. The case study below illustrates that analytics can yield a huge competitive advantage even for small and medium-sized enterprises (SMEs).

CASE STUDY

THE RIGHT CHAIR #1
Marketing Analytics Gives SMEs a Competitive Advantage

Analytical marketing is not very common in small and medium-size enterprises in the business-to-business sector. As such, if we had a model or decision support system to enable us to decide how to allocate resources across communication activities and channels, we will have a huge advantage compared to our competitors. —LEON SUIJKERBUIJK, CEO OF INOFEC BV

Inofec BV is a family-run European office furniture supplier that operates in the Netherlands and Belgium. Founded in 1986 by the current CEO's father, the company has grown into a medium-sized firm with about eighty employees. The company shows average annual growth of about 20 percent. Their more than 8,000 customers are professional end users and can choose from an array of over 7,000 SKUs.

Inofec's main goal is to offer goods of high value at low prices. Their mantra: Treat everyone as you want to be treated yourself. Their competitive advantage is adding a high level of service to their products (e.g., advice, assembly, and customized solutions) and having their own distribution network. Their service is to deliver the products to their customers, assemble the furniture, and only leave if the furniture is ready to use and the customer 100 percent satisfied. Furthermore, they spend a considerable marketing budget even during the recession, unlike their competitors, whose reaction to the recession has been focused on slashing costs drastically—including layoffs and reorganization. In the words of Leon: "Our competitors have an internal focus: management by fear regarding preservation of jobs is key."

Within a challenging business-to-business environment, Leon realized that more insights could be gained from analyzing Inofec's own financial and marketing data. He sees the recession not as a threat, but rather as an opportunity to invest in order to reap the benefits down the road. Leon is convinced that quantifying how customers move through the purchase funnel (i.e., information, evaluation, purchase)—and how marketing helps in this process—may lead to a sustainable competitive advantage. Prior to a dashboard implementation, the effectiveness of marketing communications activities was monitored by observing subsequent sales changes—without considering long-term effects, cross-effects between channels, or controlling for other factors influencing sales. Allocation decisions were mainly based on gut feel or "that's how we did it the last time." Against this background, Leon was looking for another perspective and was willing to adopt a marketing science approach.

The main marketing challenge facing Inofec is quantifying the impact of marketing communications activities on purchase funnel stages (online and offline), and ultimately its impact on profits. With this knowledge, then, they can reallocate the marketing communications budget accordingly. To this end, a dashboard tool was developed to answer the following specific questions:

- Do Inofec's marketing communications activities only "feed the funnel" or do they also have an effect on later stages of the purchase funnel?

- What is the (net) profit effect of their marketing communication activities? Especially, what is the effect of "customer-initiated contacts" versus "firm-initiated contacts"?

> ➤ When does the effect of marketing communications "hit in" and how long does it last?
>
> ➤ How can Inofec improve its profits by reallocating its marketing budgets?

Answering questions like these can lead to an improved understanding of the role of marketing communications activities and planning of appropriate strategic actions. Throughout this book, you will learn about how Inofec overcame obstacles along the journey, including database creation, dashboard implementation, and the design of a field experiment that demonstrated a fourteen-fold profit increase over the status quo.

WHAT IS A MARKETING ANALYTICS DASHBOARD?

Just like your car's dashboard, a marketing analytics dashboard brings the firm's key market-based metrics into a single display. It provides a concise set of interconnected performance drivers to be viewed in common throughout the organization.

Inofec's dashboard is shown in Figure 1–1. It is but one example of what a dashboard might look like. Hundreds of alternative designs are available at dashboardspy.com, and Chapter 11 helps you to choose among them to fit your needs best.

Let's break down the key elements of the dashboard definition:

> ➤ **Concise set:** A dashboard's purpose is to help users focus their attention on a few metrics. However, different users often focus on different metrics (typically the ones they can influence and/or that they are evaluated against), and some people are comfortable with more metrics than others, much like an airplane pilot navigates a bigger dashboard than a car driver does. Dashboards solve this issue by allowing users to customize the display to the user's preferences and to "drill down" to different page views with more detailed metrics.

Figure 1–1, Marketing Dashboard Prototype

Period	Flyers	Faxes	Adwords	Discount
1	0	400	100	7
2	0	0	50	7
3	0	0	50	7
4	4000	0	100	7
5	0	0	100	7
6	0	0	100	7
7	0	400	100	7
8	0	0	100	7
9	0	0	50	7
10	0	0	50	7
11	4000	0	100	7
12	0	0	100	7
13	0	0	100	7
14	0	0	100	7

Total Profits: $333,068.88

> **Interconnected:** A simple scorecard of metrics does not make a marketing analytics dashboard: The dashboard should help users understand how the business works and how their (proposed) actions can change the (predicted) performance! To this end, a dashboard needs an underlying (back-office) model that connects the metrics. In the Inofec dashboard shown in Figure 1–1, the user changes the marketing inputs and watches the projected profits (based on the analytics) change in real time. The next case study, "Cars: From Begging HQ to Talking Trade-Offs," illustrates the importance of the analytics dashboard for a major car company. Just like car drivers, dashboard users need to know what happens when they hit the brakes or shift gears, but they don't need to know exactly how the engine operates under the hood. Still, the existence of the engine is crucial.

> **Key performance drivers:** The presented metrics have been shown to be important, leading indicators of performance, either by experience and/or by scientific testing in the underlying model. We have seen many cases in which managers got obsessed with metrics that did not drive

results. A good dashboard refocuses its users on the metrics that truly matter.

- **To be viewed:** Dashboards visualize information through devices such as gauges, charts, and tables, often color-coded for easy summarization.

- **In common throughout the organization:** A dashboard makes it easy to share information and to get all stakeholders on the same page (often literally). There's still plenty of room for discussion on how to interpret the facts and what to do next, but at least it is clear what the facts are. Many companies also share dashboard views with partners such as suppliers, agencies, and customers, which helps to align the supply chain around common goals.

Integration Is King

Integration is key to each of the elements above, and is the clear but tough-to-achieve answer in today's challenging times. Organizations need integration on at least three levels:

1. **Data.** Understanding the firm's market and its position within the market requires information and data from diverse sources at different levels of aggregation and covering different time periods. The dashboard provides a common organizing framework.

2. **Processes.** The dashboard helps management relate inputs, such as marketing expenditures, to measures of market performance, such as market share and sales and ultimately of financial performance, such as profits, cash flows, and shareholder value, thus building a bridge between internal and external reporting.

3. **Viewpoints.** Whether assessing the market, performance, or planning, a dashboard allows different executives, in different departments and locations, to share the same, equally measured input (i.e., to view the firm's market situation in the same light).

Why Integration Is Lacking in So Many Organizations

At one extreme, different systems and departments often use their own metrics, based on their own data, processes, and viewpoints. How can marketing and finance agree if they don't speak the same language? At the other extreme, some companies wrongly believe in one "silver bullet" metric that captures all that is important.[6] A single metric may have worked, for example, for an encyclopedia salesman, selling a single durable product on commission while facing little local competition. For organizations, however, the evidence is clear: The silver bullet metric is an illusion. Organizations have both short-term and long-term interests; they need to consider both qualitative and quantitative information and must be able to differentiate the performance impact of their own actions from the influences of the environment.

In sum, a marketing analytics dashboard:

- Offers integration of diverse business activities, some of them qualitative, with performance outcomes.
- Measures both the short-term results of marketing and the long-term health of the marketing asset.
- Isolates the effects of marketing actions from the other influences on corporate performance.

CASE STUDY

CARS
From Begging HQ to Talking Trade-Offs

At a major car company in the United States, managers were dreading their meeting with foreign headquarters (HQ). The typical meeting included setting higher (stretch) targets for sales and profits in the coming years, while lowering marketing budgets. The boiling point was HQ's decision to slow down the typical development cycle by a year. "How can we reach higher sales with less advertising and older cars" was the U.S. branch's objection. However, management protest was waved away by HQ: "Everyone has to work harder and smarter.

Why can't you reach your targets?" Unfortunately, U.S. management had strong gut feelings, but no way to demonstrate how much older models and lower ad budgets would weigh on profits!

Management and I set out on a dashboard project to investigate, quantify, and visualize profit performance drivers at the annual level, to aid in the yearly budget negotiations with HQ. Several meetings with management and a study of available sources on the industry and competitors revealed dozens of potential key performance indicators (KPIs). We selected from among these KPIs the metrics that led profit and explained most of its change over time, and used them to build our econometric model (see Chapter 8). To keep the project's output at the strategic level, we summed up tactical executions and platforms (paid search, Twitter, Facebook, etc.) to the marketing instrument level (in the category "online marketing communications"). The final model explained annual profit by:

1. Average model age.
2. Offline marketing communications.
3. Online marketing communications.
4. Regular price.
5. Financial consumer incentives.
6. Nonfinancial consumer incentives (free add-ons).
7. Financial incentives by the two closest competitors.
8. External factors such as seasonality and economic climate.

The model showed excellent fit and we validated it in two ways. First, management discussed the findings within the company to ensure "face validity." Second, we set apart the last year of data as a "hold-out sample" and showed the predictive validity of our model beyond the data used to estimate it. Once these validations created buy-in, we used the model estimates to create two simple Excel tools: the scrollbar (or slide bar, as we call it) shown in Figure 1-2 and the heat map shown in Figure 1-3. (To more fully appreciate the heat map, you will want to see it in color; you can find it on my website: notthesizeofthedata.com.)

Managers enjoyed the ability to try out different scenarios, both by moving the scrollbars and observing the predicted profit outcome

Figure 1–2, Slide Bars for Manipulating Marketing Variables

Change the levels of the marketing variables to see how the profits change.

Profits | 4.775

Marketing Variables

		Slide Bars
Product age (months)	12.00	◀ ▶
Price	15.00	◀ ▶
TV ads	2,005	◀ ▶
Online ads	200	◀ ▶
Distribution share	20	◀ ▶

and by focusing on changing two marketing inputs at a time to observe the best profit that the model could achieve in the heat map. Key to dashboard acceptance and use was the (correct!) feeling that the model did not replace the decision maker by providing a single "optimal" or "right" answer, but that it helped the decision maker by running what-if analyses (e.g., "If the average model age increases by one year, how much do our incentives have to increase to achieve the same profit level?" and "What happens if we increase the communication budget instead?").

The dashboard tools also allowed the more involved user to "unhide" the Excel columns that show the model estimates and to question or change them. Indeed, headquarters did not simply "roll over" when presented with evidence that profits would drop by 20 percent on the combination of older car models and lower ad budgets (while the target profit was 10 percent higher). Instead, they demanded the detailed econometric evidence including the predictive performance in the hold-out sample. This changed the discussion from a general "you just have to work harder and smarter" to the specific trade-offs managers face and how to join forces to overcome them. One interesting outcome: The low average profit effect of an often-used activity challenged common wisdom and encouraged managers to give creative employees more latitude to think further outside the box in that area. In the end, a new marketing plan was adopted with substantially higher spending on some items, lower spending on others—and smarter use of the same budget for the remainder. Profit exceeded even the stretch target the next year.

Figure 1–3, Heat Map of the Interaction of Two Marketing Variables on Profits

TV advertising in thousands of $ \ Price in $	10	15	20	25	30	35	40	45	50	55	60	65	70	75
0	0.02	1.04	1.92	2.64	3.22	3.65	3.93	4.06	4.04	3.87	3.56	3.09	2.47	1.71
250	0.65	1.68	2.56	3.28	3.86	4.29	4.57	4.70	4.68	4.51	4.19	3.73	3.11	2.35
500	1.25	2.27	3.15	3.87	4.45	4.88	5.16	5.29	5.27	5.10	4.79	4.32	3.70	2.94
750	1.79	2.81	3.69	4.41	4.99	5.42	5.70	5.83	5.81	5.64	5.33	4.86	4.24	3.48
1000	2.28	3.30	4.18	4.91	5.48	5.91	6.19	6.32	6.30	6.13	5.82	5.35	4.73	3.97
1250	2.72	3.74	4.62	5.35	5.92	6.35	6.63	6.76	6.74	6.58	6.26	5.79	5.18	4.41
1500	3.11	4.13	5.01	5.74	6.32	6.74	7.02	7.15	7.13	6.97	6.65	6.18	5.57	4.80
1750	3.45	4.48	5.35	6.08	6.66	7.09	7.37	7.50	7.48	7.31	6.99	6.52	5.91	5.14
2000	3.74	4.77	5.65	6.37	6.95	7.38	7.66	7.79	7.77	7.60	7.28	6.82	6.20	5.44
2250	3.99	5.01	5.89	6.62	7.19	7.62	7.90	8.03	8.01	7.84	7.53	7.06	6.44	5.68
2500	4.18	5.21	6.08	6.81	7.39	7.81	8.09	8.22	8.21	8.04	7.72	7.25	6.64	5.87
2750	4.32	5.35	6.23	6.95	7.53	7.96	8.24	8.37	8.35	8.18	7.86	7.40	6.78	6.02
3000	4.42	5.44	6.32	7.05	7.62	8.05	8.33	8.46	8.44	8.27	7.96	7.49	6.88	6.11
3250	4.46	5.49	6.36	7.09	7.67	8.10	8.38	8.51	8.49	8.32	8.00	7.54	6.92	6.15
3500	4.46	5.48	6.36	7.09	7.66	8.09	8.37	8.50	8.48	8.31	8.00	7.53	6.91	6.15
3750	4.40	5.43	6.30	7.03	7.61	8.04	8.32	8.45	8.43	8.26	7.94	7.48	6.86	6.09
4000	4.30	5.32	6.20	6.93	7.50	7.93	8.21	8.34	8.32	8.15	7.84	7.37	6.75	5.99
4250	4.14	5.17	6.04	6.77	7.35	7.78	8.06	8.19	8.17	8.00	7.68	7.22	6.60	5.84
4500	3.94	4.97	5.84	6.57	7.15	7.57	7.85	7.98	7.97	7.80	7.48	7.01	6.40	5.63
4750	3.69	4.71	5.59	6.32	6.89	7.32	7.60	7.73	7.71	7.54	7.23	6.76	6.14	5.38
5000	3.38	4.41	5.29	6.01	6.59	7.02	7.30	7.43	7.41	7.24	6.92	6.46	5.84	5.08

WHY MARKETING ANALYTICS DASHBOARDS?

Marketing analytics dashboards respond to the increasing complexity and diversity of marketing data faced by senior management in the information age—of which the Cars case study is just one example. In our experience across industries and firms, managers mention at least four factors driving the need for dashboards: poor data organization, managerial bias, increasing pressure on marketing, and the need for cross-departmental integration.

Poor Organization

Data overload is obvious in the fragmentation of media, multichannel management, and the proliferation of product lines and services. Information technology makes it possible for firms to collect and analyze data on customer activities across touch points and channels.

Unisys, for example, gathers hundreds of metrics generated by brand tracking, CRM programs, tradeshows, media reports, satisfaction studies, and blogs. Service- and contract-based markets always give firms individual-level data, but online tracking of browsing use now does so for virtually any company. This proliferation requires greater data organization as indicated in the successful examples of the "information-based strategy" at Capital One or "information-based customer management" at Barclays Bank.[7]

Managerial Bias

Human processing capacities remain limited, and research has demonstrated the presence and danger of managerial biases arising from shortcuts in information processing and decision making.[8] For example, managers anchor their new decisions based on old decisions and do not adjust enough based on incoming information. The result is that brands and regions that got large marketing budgets in the past will continue to get large budgets, even if the money is now more useful elsewhere.

Firms that see analytic capabilities as a key element of their strategy outperform their peers since they know what products their customers want, what prices those customers will pay, how many items each will buy, and what triggers will make people buy more.

Increasing Pressure on Marketing

CEOs, CFOs, and CMOs demand more accountability from the marketing department. Marketing is challenged both to drive growth and to keep costs under control, with the immediate focus on either objective swinging with the business cycle. Broad surveys of marketing and nonmarketing professionals consistently reveal increased expectations regarding marketing accountability as well as its effect on the marketing department's influence within a company.[9]

The goals of the typical marketing department have been revealed as disconnected from companies' leadership agendas. As a result, CMOs are advised to agree on a "marketing contract" with the CEO that specifies exactly which metrics marketing is supposed to improve. In this regard, a dashboard helps ensure everyone is "on the same page" to detect and discuss marketing successes and failures.

The Need for Cross-Departmental Integration

The ability of marketing to reach across functions to accomplish company goals is an increasingly important determinant of its success. Many firms have integrated marketing, innovation, and strategic growth leadership into a single corporate function.[10] Companies facing disruptive cross-national mergers and global expansion especially need integration. This brings together marketing departments with different values, performance metrics, and reporting practices. Standardized tools and processes for efficiency are key to driving growth in such organizations.

WHO USES MARKETING ANALYTICS DASHBOARDS?

The benefits of marketing analytics dashboards are relevant to companies of any size and in any kind of industry. This book provides dozens of case studies in companies ranging from sixty employees to hundreds of thousands and in industries ranging from fast-moving consumer goods to online travel. In the broader area of dashboards (not necessarily connected to analytics), the footnotes for this chapter list over 200 companies, including:

- Business communication (Avaya, Cisco)
- Consumer credit (Capital One)
- Education (Montgomery County Public Schools of Rockville, Maryland)
- Fast-moving consumer goods (Heineken)
- Gaming (Harrah's)
- Government (Connecticut Economic Dashboard, Atlanta Dashboard)
- Hospitality (Hilton)
- Investment banking (Morgan Stanley)
- Mutual funds (Vanguard)
- Online services (Google)
- Systems integration (Unisys)
- Technology (SAP)
- Transportation (Virginia)
- TV broadcasting (British Sky)

As to who within these companies uses dashboards, users come from all management levels. We have seen dashboards used by CEOs, CMOs, CFOs, and COOs; by brand managers, marketing specialists, production managers, and R&D managers; by the sales force, you name it.

HOW CAN A MARKETING ANALYTICS DASHBOARD HELP YOU?

A marketing analytics dashboard can help you in several ways. In particular, they help you provide better and faster answers to typical management questions:

1. What happened? Dashboards enable consistent measurements and regular monitoring.
2. Why did it happen? Analytics dashboards relate management action to key performance indicators and hard performance.
3. What will happen if? Analytics dashboards enable what-if analysis to predict the perfomance outcomes of alternative scenarios and plans.
4. What should happen? Analytics dashboards allow you to optimize or at least improve decisions and communicate this process more transparently.

Several well-known companies have experienced these benefits.

A dashboard *enforces consistency* in measures and measurement procedures across departments and business units. For example, Avaya operates in over fifty countries and diverse markets, with varying marketing tactics. Before the dashboard project, the company had no commonality of systems around the globe (limiting data gathering), different definitions of what constitutes a "qualified lead" (a key performance metric in the hand-off from marketing to sales for business-to-business companies), and a lack of regional interest in gathering metrics.[11]

A dashboard helps to *monitor performance*. Monitoring in turn may be both evaluative (who or what performed well?) and developmental (what have we learned?). Google provides a good example: Dashboard metrics are early indicators of performance, and if a dip occurs in, for example, the "trust and privacy" metric, the company takes corrective action.[12]

A dashboard may be used to *plan* (what should our goals and strategies be for the future given where we are now?). For example, Ameritrade started with corporate scorecards from the strategic planning department to develop a dashboard that plugs in to the planning cycle and is tied to quarterly compensation.[13]

A dashboard may be used to *communicate to important stakeholders*. In particular, it communicates not only what the performance is, but also communicates what an organization values as performance by the choice of metrics on the dashboard. Vanguard has had great success in communicating dashboard metrics to its corporate board, and also in translating their business focus on customer loyalty, feedback, and word-of-mouth into their measurement on the dashboard.[14]

A dashboard offers a great *starting point for tough discussions*, such as at the annual budgeting cycle, when the going gets tough (recessions, product recalls), and/or when management sets stretch targets without providing the necessary resources. The case study "Cars: From Begging HQ to Talking Trade-Offs" above offers a wonderful example in the car industry, where marketing analytics quantified the relation between marketing actions and profits. The dashboard allows easy what-if analyses to discuss trade-offs with foreign headquarters. It also enables more effective communication with marketing partners, especially as companies move to performance-based compensation of agency work. The case study "Not All Fun and EB Games" in Chapter 4 is an excellent illustration of this benefit.

WRAP-UP AND MANAGER'S MEMO

Marketing analytics dashboards play a vital ongoing role in marketing and business decisions for leading companies. As these best practices show, dashboards can help managers boost both accountability and creativity for better marketing performance. In the words of CMOs at Target, Fidelity, MasterCard, and H&R Block, "Science enriches the art in marketing, and art accelerates the science." If the art means "asking the right questions to create winning strategies," science is "using data and analytics to answer questions, inform decisions and optimize marketing efforts."[15] This is our goal and invitation for you in this book. We close with a checklist of questions to diagnose your organization on the need for a marketing analytics dashboard—do share it with your boss!

MANAGER'S MEMO

DO YOU NEED A MARKETING ANALYTICS DASHBOARD?

Is your organization or team suffering from any of the following?

- ❑ Trust issues between marketing and finance executives?

- ❑ Lack of real-time employee insight in how they are progressing to achieve firm goals?

- ❑ Confusion about the effectiveness of new media (what is your social media ROI)?

- ❑ Lack of comparable metrics across media (online vs. offline) or countries?

- ❑ Too many "key performance indicators" without proof of their sales impact?

- ❑ "You are too young / too old to understand" (authority instead of fact-based arguments)?

- ❑ Resource competition between online and offline marketing without clear attribution?

Can you or your marketing department answer these tough questions on accountability?

- ❑ If we need to cut 20 percent from our marketing budget, what would we cut?

- ❑ If we need to obtain 10 percent more revenues next year, where would they come from?

- ❑ What is affecting our current and future performance, and by how much?

- ❑ When does our marketing action affect performance, and how long does it last?

- ❑ Which marketing action gets us the highest return on investment and where?

❑ Can we increase baseline performance with a one-shot or with a sustained campaign?

❑ How can we improve the efficiency of effective media and the effectiveness of efficient media?

Do you want to be able to do the following?

❑ Have the facts at everyone's fingertips so meetings focus on productive plans to action?

❑ Justify your budgets and proposed changes in the winning financial language?

❑ Scale up creative and sales-driving campaigns quickly?

❑ Deploy marketing analytics to turn data into better decisions in your firm?

❑ Leverage local learning worldwide with globally agreed-upon metrics?

❑ Predict customer and competitive reactions to proposed marketing plans?

❑ Reward managers who help move prospects down online and offline funnels?

If you have answered "yes" to any of the above questions, this book is for you!

CHAPTER 2

Compare the Marketing Analytics Dashboard to Your Current Scoring System

A common pitfall in the data-driven journey is more emphasis on reporting than deep-dive analysis. The analytics team's time is primarily spent on maintaining the existing reports and responding to ad-hoc reporting requests. Almost no emphasis is placed on advanced analysis, which can provide significantly more value to the business.

—BRENT DYKES, EVANGELIST FOR CUSTOMER ANALYTICS, ADOBE

CHANCES ARE YOU'VE HEARD ABOUT key performance indicators (KPIs), balanced scorecards, and dashboards. Maybe you've been using these tools and are disappointed by their ability to improve your decisions. As one manager said to me in a recent seminar: "We have reports for about thirty key performance indicators, but nobody has a clue how each KPI increases profits. In meetings, we overfocus on the few KPIs that happen to be low this week, instead of seeing the forest through the trees. We desperately need an engine behind the dashboard: analytics on how marketing affects performance."

Let's make sure that we speak a common language and can compare analytics dashboards with related, but different tools. Specifically we will look at reporting dashboards, balanced scorecards, and key performance indicators. As a result, you will know an analytics dashboard when you see one!

REPORTING VERSUS ANALYTICS IN DASHBOARDS

As you recall from Chapter 1, we see a marketing analytics dashboard as a concise set of interconnected performance drivers to be viewed in common throughout the organization.

"Connected" means that we have a link between one metric and another; for example, we know that, on average, doubling the TV advertising budget leads to a 10 percent increase in sales. However, many reporting tools are touted as dashboards without connecting key performance metrics. They are good-looking reporting tools (i.e., neat graphic displays) that enable users to see and analyze performance information at a glance.

Finally, analytics dashboards contain both short- and long-term business performance metrics. They are not simply operational tools to manage day-to-day problems. A good example of an operational tool is the CitiStat program in Baltimore, Maryland. In developing this program, Mayor Martin J. O'Malley "sought to build the kind of information management and control system that would enhance the capacity of city agencies to identify, respond to, and anticipate problems as they were emerging."[1] CitiStat employs geographic mapping tools to track activity measures (e.g., animal carcasses collected, missed garbage pickups) across the city. In this sense, CitiStat—like its analogue CompStat used by police departments around the country—is an operations-management tool that provides managers with nearly real-time data on departmental activities. The utility of these systems rests largely in day-to-day operations management, where data can be used to respond immediately to problems identified on the ground by rapidly redeploying resources. While these tools are useful for managers, they generally do not establish targets for strategic outcomes—nor do they track performance against those targets.

The beauty of an analytics dashboard lies in its ability to integrate reporting and analytics, short-term and long-term data, and tactical and strategic decision tools. In contrast to Baltimore's CitiStat, the Atlanta Dashboard used in the city of Atlanta, Georgia, illustrates customization to meet specific business needs of a whole company or any of its divisions. The dashboard team realized that, while it admired analytics dashboards in the private sector, their strong focus on profits did not fit the needs of a local government. The City of Atlanta is like a conglomerate spanning fifteen different lines of business, each with a different culture peculiar to the highly specialized nature of that business. Moreover, private sector dashboards are typically "shielded from the public eye,"[2] which does not meet Atlanta's needs for public access. So, the team decided to go with a dashboard that would fit the needs of Atlanta's municipal government (see the next case study). With the dashboard, Atlanta achieved its internal management goals—and provided meaningful public access. That is what we mean when we say that dashboards can be very flexible and highly customizable. In fact, a dashboard's ability to be tailored to specific needs of a particular (we would say any!) environment makes it different from a scorecard. But let's have a closer look at both of them.

MARKETING ANALYTICS DASHBOARDS AND BALANCED SCORECARDS

In many companies I work with, I need to discuss the difference between a dashboard and a scorecard or, more accurately, the Balanced Scorecard. Let us first speak about the Balanced Scorecard as a predecessor of the marketing analytic dashboard—and then about understanding the difference between the two.

Originally the Balanced Scorecard was developed by Kaplan and Norton[3] in 1992 to serve as a business performance management tool that allowed alignment of business practices with the overall strategy of an organization. The Balanced Scorecard views business from four distinct perspectives, united around a company's common strategy and vision (see Figure 2–1).

Further, each perspective includes goals defined by the company in line with its strategy and vision, and measures selected by the company to track its actual business performance. In this way the Balanced

Figure 2–1, The Balanced Scorecard by Kaplan and Norton

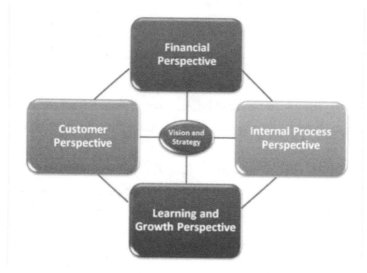

Scorecard allows senior management to monitor and measure the success of any business, predominantly shaped by customer satisfaction, operational and financial efficiency and effectiveness, and the ability of an organization to learn and evolve. As a replacement of traditional accounting measures, the Balanced Scorecard deserves the attention of business researchers and practitioners. Moreover, it includes the customer perspective, which is key to businesses and to dashboards. Unfortunately, it does not reflect the depth of marketing thinking for a silly reason: Kaplan and Norton invited marketing specialists to help develop the Balanced Scorecard, but none of them showed up!

How can the Balanced Scorecard experience help you in the upgrade to a marketing analytics dashboard? Well, they share a lot of common ground.

First, Kaplan and Norton defined the Balanced Scorecard as a set of measures that provides top managers with a quick and comprehensive view of a business. It demonstrates financial results of actions taken and presumably indicates the drivers of future performance. A dashboard, too, provides a snapshot of current performance of a business. Further, a marketing analytics dashboard is also aimed at aligning marketing objectives with a company's strategy, and it does also link inputs (marketing expenditures) with outputs (effects or financial results of marketing actions). Even the imagery is the same: Just as our "dashboard" terminology derives from a vehicle dashboard, Kaplan and Norton compare the Balanced Scorecard with an airplane cockpit. Both pilots and senior managers need detailed information on diverse aspects of a flight and business, respectively, and an airplane cockpit as well as the Balanced Scorecard provides the most critical information integrated from different data sources into a single summary screen.

The difference between the Balanced Scorecard—*a* balanced scorecard—and the marketing analytics dashboard becomes apparent once you consider applying one of the approaches and dig deeper below the surface of the two terms. While a balanced scorecard is a standard framework, the marketing analytics dashboard is a highly customizable model to measure and improve business performance. For example, dashboards can be used at any level of organizational hierarchy. They integrate both short- and long-term objectives of a firm—or of any given level in the organizational hierarchy. Scorecards, on the other hand, are more focused on long-term deliverables and not very effective at tracking operational measures that need quick access and reaction. To sum up, scorecards and dashboards mainly differ along the following three dimensions:

1. **Performance measurement vs. performance management.** A balanced scorecard is only concerned with progress toward strategic company objectives. It displays periodic snapshots of performance related to an organization's strategic objectives and goals. In contrast, a properly designed and executed dashboard links to systems that track ongoing (often real-time) performance and warns its users when performance against metrics deviates from the preestablished target.

2. **Standardization vs. customizability.** The dashboard integrates short- and long-term objectives, while a balanced

scorecard typically focuses on long-term performance and strategic business indicators. In this way, a balanced scorecard lacks flexibility. Although it contains diverse measures, it categorizes these metrics within the framework of four perspectives. A dashboard, on the other hand, does not limit itself to a predefined number of perspectives or viewpoints, and can be fully tailored to the needs and interests of a specific company. Although a balanced scorecard does include a customer perspective, it is rather weak on consumer perceptions, and very little attention is given to competition. With a dashboard, the company can choose the specific metrics that drive its performance most—as detailed in Chapter 7 and Chapter 8.

3. **Top management–focused vs. applies at all organizational levels.** A balanced scorecard predominantly targets top and senior management, while a dashboard can be applied and used at any level of organizational hierarchy.

In practice, however, the line between scorecards and dashboards is frequently blurred, and very often companies will find themselves labeling a dashboard approach as a scorecard and vice versa. If it helps you in your organization, feel free to call your marketing performance system a scorecard or a dashboard. What matters is that the system functions as you want it to, that it uses the right metrics in the right way, and that it gets buy-in throughout the organization. Also, a balanced scorecard and an analytics dashboard are not competitors; rather, they can complement each other. The scorecard provides a universal framework to manage business health of an organization, while a dashboard offers an integrated tool that allows tracking as well as managing both the short- and long-term business performance of a company.

Now let's take a closer look at the *differences* between the Atlanta Dashboard and Charlotte's Balanced Scorecard in the case study that follows.[4]

- -

CITY PERFORMANCE
From Charlotte's Balanced Scorecard to Atlanta's Dashboard

In early 2002, the City of Atlanta introduced a new performance measurement system for municipal government. The system was intended to:

➤ Provide accurate and timely information about the state of city services and operations.

➤ Provide management with operating targets and a means of tracking progress toward those targets in order to increase management accountability.

➤ Provide a public window into the city's operating environment in order to increase transparency, thereby regaining the public's confidence in the competence of the city government.

With these objectives in mind, the mayor's team began by examining the performance measurement systems used by other governments. Their experiences were very insightful.

On the other hand, Charlotte, North Carolina, was the highest-profile U.S. city at the time to adopt a balanced scorecard. While reporting an overall positive assessment of the system, Charlotte found adoption—and adaptation—of its Balanced Scorecard to be extremely time-consuming, as it focused on internal processes. Atlanta sidestepped some of that time commitment by focusing on outcome measures, not on internal business processes. Atlanta officials saw uncertain connections between some of the internal process and outcome measures as seen from the eyes of the public included in the Charlotte Balanced Scorecard. They also noticed the potential for internal process perspectives to vary among departments. Learning from Charlotte's experience, the project team designed the Atlanta Dashboard to be both streamlined and useful.

For one, it was important to ensure that measures could be weighted to reflect their priority. In the area of public safety, for example, the dimensions may include (1) reducing crime, (2) reducing fire loss, and (3) rehabilitating criminals, but reducing crime has a higher weight due to its greater importance in contributing to public safety. Moreover, within the area of crime reduction, specific crimes (such as homicide) may be weighted more heavily. Those weights may change over time as the city's strategic priorities evolve.

The Dashboard can also be expanded vertically. Building on the example from the police department, the geographic zones that interest the mayor can be divided and subdivided to allow the police chief to track measures in more discrete units. The Dashboard can, in fact, be driven down throughout the organization, perhaps ultimately to personalized dashboards for each individual contributor.

In addition, the Dashboard makes links and dependencies among departments visible to senior managers. Street cleaning provides a good example of this. Public works managers complain that streets are not clean because the large, mechanical street sweepers have not been repaired in a timely manner by the city's Department of Motor Transport Services. Department management counters that the vehicles are abused (by the drivers) and are therefore out of service more than they should be. Without a way of measuring the performance of either operation, a stalemate ensued. The Dashboard helped to resolve the issue. The relevant outcome goals include (1) reported citizen satisfaction with street cleanliness and (2) departmental records on miles of streets swept. Both are shaped by the availability of street sweepers, which in turn is driven in part by the maintenance and repair of the street sweeper fleet. Maintenance and repair link street sweeping to the Department of Motor Transport Services, which, in collaboration with the public works function, has developed the goals of (1) 100 percent turnaround within twenty-four hours of all street sweepers receiving preventive maintenance, and (2) 100 percent turnaround within two weeks of all street sweepers receiving major repairs. In turn, the department reports "abnormal failures" due to operator abuse or the failure to bring the vehicles in for preventative maintenance. The combination of these measures allows senior management on both sides to track performance and to hold everyone accountable.

Finally, the Atlanta Dashboard is actively used in weekly meetings of the mayor's cabinet to review performance reports. Each week the performance of selected departments is reviewed against the departmental plan, with programmatic changes formulated as necessary to address shortfalls. Those presentations and discussions help in interpreting the data, in targeting performance problems, and in refining the Dashboard. As that description suggests, the Dashboard remains a work in progress, with performance measures evolving as departments adapt to the system.

In sum, the Atlanta Dashboard embodies several attributes of a true and useful dashboard; it is:

- Strategic and operational: Measurement focuses on outcomes rather than inputs or outputs, and it links directly to the city's core business strategies.

- Evolving and dynamic, not static: As the city's strategic priorities evolve, so too can the measurement system.

- Participatory and iterative, not top-down in development: While the ultimate responsibility for what to measure resides with top management, input was and is solicited from all levels of the hierarchy, both to maximize information and to build ownership.

- Tightly hierarchical, not loosely distributed in administration: The system is administered in a traditional hierarchical, pyramid format so that the work of individual supervisors and contributors can be linked directly to performance expectations higher in the pyramid.

- Transparent, not opaque: The system is relatively easy to understand, even for someone with little knowledge of city government, such as the average Atlanta resident.

DECISION SUPPORT TOOLS AND MARKETING MIX MODELS

Marketing analytics dashboards are part of the broad class of decision support systems that provide managers with guidance on marketing decisions, such as advertising, promotional activity, and sales force allocation. We see dashboards as a combination of individual decision support systems, which concentrate on integration and alignment at the company level rather than on an individual activity level. In his classic paper on useful models, Little defines a marketing decision support system as "a coordinated collection of data, systems, tools, and techniques with supporting software and hardware by which an organization gathers and interprets relevant information from business and environment and turns it into a basis for marketing action."[5]

Marketing analytics dashboards meet this definition. The dashboard display is the graphical user interface that is the output of a larger system of supporting software and hardware. This support may include multiple databases and multiple models that connect the dots between marketing activities and sales. Most often, these models are a form of "marketing mix models" that use "multivariate regressions on sales and marketing time series data to estimate the impact of various marketing tactics (marketing mix) on sales and then forecast the impact of future sets of tactics."[6] In the online world (discussed in Chapter 9), marketing mix models are also known as attribution models. Every model has its limitations; for example, most marketing mix models only pick up short-term effects and thus fail to consider long-term effects of advertising or word of mouth. This limitation is overcome in vector autoregressive models (see Chapter 8), for which econometrician Christopher A. Sims received the 2011 Nobel Prize for Economics. The key point, however, is that the dashboard user does not need to know the mathematics of model estimation (just as a car driver need not understand the finer workings of the engine under the hood): the dashboard display provides the few connected metrics and dials needed to assess and improve performance.

In sum, it is the integration of performance metrics with underlying drivers and processes that makes a dashboard such a powerful management tool. By making the business model explicit and linking data to the model, "properly created dashboards provide the mechanism to drive effective management and resource allocation decisions."[7]

By making key information available throughout the organization, dashboards should enable improved decisions and, ultimately, improved financial performance.

DASHBOARD BUILDING BLOCKS: METRICS AND KEY PERFORMANCE INDICATORS

It's important to speak the same language on metrics and key performance indicators (KPIs). Even if we all have a general idea of what these terms could mean, they are often used interchangeably. First, I'll define metrics, and distinguish between financial and marketing metrics, and between process and outcome metrics. Then I'll explain the distinction between a metric and a KPI.

What Is a Metric?

The American Marketing Association defines metrics as "a system of measures that helps to quantify particular characteristics."[8] So, a metric is simply a measure, and a business performance metric is a measure of a specific business activity or set of activities that contribute to, affect, and shape the overall business performance of an organization.

Business metrics can come from several sources, with finance and marketing being most relevant to measuring return on marketing investment. Table 2–1 gives an overview of metrics from finance and marketing, which have been competing for attention of dashboard developers. Academicians and practitioners are still arguing whether financial or marketing metrics are more important in a business environment. Well, it depends. The decision on metrics is largely shaped by company strategy, its orientation (e.g., market orientation), management, and environment.[9] The key conclusion of this research is that marketing metrics are equally important as financial metrics for marketing accountability.

Unfortunately, many companies undervalue the importance of marketing metrics. The financial systems of most businesses are set up to track revenues, costs, factory overhead, accounts receivable, operating expenses, and profits, but they usually overlook the fact that a business's customers are its most important asset and the one significant source of positive cash flow.[10]

While sales revenues, net profit, return on sales, etc., are important

Table 2-1, Partial List of Marketing and Financial Metrics

Marketing-Mix Activity	Marketing Metrics	Financial Metrics
General Metrics	Market share (units or dollars) Awareness (product or brand) Satisfaction (product or brand) Likeability (product or brand) Preference (product or brand) Brand imagery (brand) Willingness to recommend (product or brand) Loyalty (product or brand) Perceived product quality Consideration set Total customers Share of customer wallet Share of voice	Net profit Return on investment Return on sales Return on marketing investment Net present value Economic value added Marketing expenditures (percentage specifically on brand-building activities) Stock prices/stock returns Tobin's q Target volume (units or sales) Customer segment profitability Customer lifetime value
Traditional Advertising	Impressions Reach Recall	Cost per customer acquired/cost per thousand impressions
Internet Advertising	Impressions Hits/visits/page views Click-through rate	Lead generation Cost per click Conversion rate Internal rate of return
Direct to Consumer	Reach Number of responses by campaign New customer retention rate	Cost per customer acquired Conversion rate Lead generation
Social Media	Hits/visits/page views Number of followers/tags Volume of coverage by media	Lead generation Cost per exposure Total costs
Price Promotions	Impressions Reach Trial/repeat volume (or ratio)	Promotional sales/incremental lift Redemption rates (e.g., coupons) Internal rate of return
Pricing	Price premium Reservation price Relative price	Unit margin/margin percentage Price elasticity Optimal price
New Product Development	Belief in new product concept Attitude toward product/brand Expected annual growth rate Trial and repeat	Expected margin (%) Level of cannibalization/cannibalization rate Internal rate of return
Sales Force	Reach Number of responses by campaign New customer retention rate	Sales potential forecast Sales force productivity Sales funnel/sales pipeline
Distribution	Out-of-stock percentage/availability Strength of channel relationships Product category volume	Total inventory/total distributors Channel margins Sales per store/stock keeping units
PR/Sponsorship	Volume of coverage by media Reach Recal	Lead generation Cost per exposure

metrics of a firm's financial performance, they are backward-looking, not forward-looking. Moreover, from the financial metrics alone, we cannot tell how well a company performed relative to its competitors. Therefore, marketing decision makers should balance both marketing and financial metrics and find just the right mix of measures for their company.

Regardless of their marketing/finance origin, metrics can focus on the process or the result.

While results metrics tell your company where it stands, process metrics can tell you where it will or can achieve in the future. Because of this particular feature of process marketing measures, they are especially important for assessment of your business health. Table 2–2 lists some typical examples of both process and result metrics.[11]

What Is a Key Performance Indicator?

A key performance indicator is a special business performance metric. It is key in measuring the performance of an organization. In the marketing context, a metric is a KPI when it drives performance. For marketing these include sales, market share, profits, etc. Three critical features of KPIs are shown in Figure 2–2.

How many of the "KPIs" sold to you by (online) information vendors fit these criteria? And how do you select a few from the dozens, sometimes hundreds, of metrics that are aligned with your strategic goals? The dashboard should focus on metrics that drive performance most and that lead performance (i.e., the early warning indicators). Chapter 8 shows how to upgrade from KPIs to key leading performance indicators (KLPIs). After all, management attention and dashboard space is limited. So you'd better use it in the best way!

WRAP-UP AND MANAGER'S MEMO

To understand how a marketing analytics dashboard can improve your organization, it pays to compare it with the tools you are already using. Reporting dashboards display data in a visually pleasing way, but do

Table 2–2, Process Versus Result Metrics

Measurement Perspective	Time Perspective	
	Process Metrics	**Result Metrics**
Internal Company Metrics	Company metrics occurring during an operating period, such as: • Product defects • Late deliveries • Late payments • Inventory turnover	Company metrics reports at the end of an operating period, such as: • Sales revenues • Percent gross profit • Net profits before tax • Return on assets
External Company Metrics	Marketing metrics occurring during an operating period, such as: • Customer awareness • Customer satisfaction • Perceived performance • Intent to repurchase	Marketing metrics reports at the end of an operating period, such as: • Relative market share • Market share • Customer retention • Revenue per customer

Figure 2–2, Key Performance Indicators

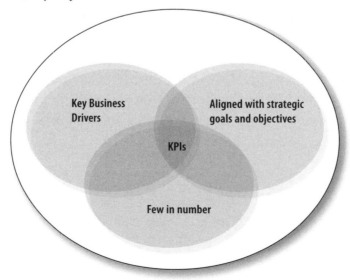

not have the analytic engine running in the background to help decision makers run scenarios and project the expected returns of marketing actions. Balanced scorecards consider metrics relevant to multiple stakeholders and offer rich inspiration on possible key performance indicators. However, they only offer the big picture and are often not actionable enough at the level of decision makers in companies and nonprofit organizations. The comparison between Charlotte's Balanced Scorecard and the Atlanta Dashboard is very informative.

As you recall from Chapter 1, a marketing analytics dashboard is a concise set of interconnected performance drivers to be viewed in common throughout the organization. Does this apply to the current decision tools in your organization? Chances are it does not. For example, only 14 percent of CMO respondents said that "everyone has the same synchronized view when they request information about a customer."[12]

Here are three key issues to keep in mind when you are reviewing your organization's tools for marketing decision makers: is your marketing performance measurement system (1) concise, (2) interconnected, and (3) organization-wide? The specific questions to be answered are:

MANAGER'S MEMO

DO YOU HAVE A MARKETING ANALYTICS DASHBOARD?

Is your current marketing performance measurement system *concise?*

☐ Does it give your boss or CEO an at a-glance overview of key business drivers?

☐ Does it distinguish inputs from in-process and outputs?

☐ Does it focus on a key few output metrics at each level of decision making?

❑ Does it focus on a few inputs the decision maker can influence at each level?

Is your current marketing performance measurement system *interconnected?*

❑ Does it connect key performance indicators to each other (as in a purchase funnel)?

❑ Does it connect marketing inputs to relevant outputs for decision makers and the firm?

❑ Does it allow decision makers to change the input and observe how outputs change?

❑ Does it integrate data analytics with data reporting in an easy-to-use interface?

Is your current marketing performance measurement system *organization-wide?*

❑ Does it apply to both senior management and context-specific decisions?

❑ Does it contain short-term and long-term metrics for tactical and strategic decisions?

❑ Is it used for performance management, not just measurement, at each decision level?

❑ Is it used in meetings and performance reviews?

PART TWO

Plan Your Marketing Analytics Dashboard

CHAPTER 3

Start with the Vision

To prove the value of their role and justify investment, CMOs must tie their marketing plans closer to business results, and engage technology and sales peers to create a consolidated vision of how to succeed with customers.

—FORRESTER RESEARCH AND HEIDRICK & STRUGGLES,
"THE EVOLVED CMO," 2012

NOW YOU KNOW WHAT MARKETING ANALYTICS dashboards can do for you, and how they are an improvement over currently used tools. Are you eager to start a dashboard to serve urgent operational needs? Be careful to first establish its strategic purpose. Operations should be aligned with a company's formulated strategy and vision. Everything starts with the vision—it's the foundation for a strategy that translates into day-to-day operations.

Your dashboard requires a similar vision. A clear understanding of the firm's strategic objectives and priorities is the paramount prerequisite for the project's success and will form a solid basis for a dashboard development and implementation. The challenge at this stage is twofold: setting the project's goals in line with the firm's strategy, and communicating these goals convincingly throughout the organization.

In this chapter we take a closer look at issues that may occur at the initial stage of a dashboard project and suggest workable solutions.

BUSINESS STRATEGY DRIVES THE DASHBOARD

The single most important basic characteristic of an analytics dashboard is that it be aligned with corporate goals. *Why* is alignment with the company's strategy so important? Think of the metrics your car's dashboard displays. What if instead of a speedometer and fuel gauge your dashboard contained information on daily oil prices? While this might be interesting to know, it wouldn't tell you how well your vehicle is doing and what you need to do to keep it going. It's as inappropriate as measuring jumping height of a swimmer. Likewise, if a company's dashboard does not include any customer-related metrics, it is simply inconsistent with the company's strategy and vision. Such a dashboard will not reflect the company's progress toward its strategic objectives, and it will not uncover pitfalls and gaps in the company's strategy as well as execution.

A dashboard should integrate relevant metrics, consistent with a firm's business and corporate strategy. Displayed data should not just be interesting, but relevant to the decision at hand so it can help improve performance. In a word, the dashboard that does not fit with the firm's strategy is a waste of time and resources. Consider the Unisys dashboard experience, discussed in the case study that follows.[1]

CASE STUDY

UNISYS MAKES GOAL ALIGNMENT A KEY PRIORITY

Unisys is a global information technology services and solutions company. Before its dashboard launch, there was no single system to measure return on marketing investment (ROMI). The dashboard team faced several challenges:

> Prior to the dashboard initiative, the company's marketing activities across the countries were not measured, not reported, or not reported in a coordinated or timely manner.

> Corporate and marketing managers at Unisys were not able to evaluate both the marketing's role in generating and delivering value to the company and its performance.

> Management had limited ability to identify inefficiencies, redundancies, and activities that did not create value for the business.

This situation was further complicated by the complexity of the company's organizational structure. Marketing budgets were controlled and managed within six separate organizations. Each organization defined their own strategies and set supporting priorities and goals. Unisys resolved these issues through the marketing dashboard implementation, as it provided the company with a vehicle to tackle its marketing challenges and validate the strategic importance of marketing.

Now, the big part of the marketing dashboard's success at Unisys lies in its alignment with the company's overall strategic objectives. In fact, Unisys indicated goal alignment as one of the seven key operating parameters it agreed upon prior to the dashboard initiative's start. Once Unysis had ensured that all important goals, objectivities, activities, and metrics were aligned, it was able to achieve the following strategically important results:

> A common set of goals and objectives for the marketing function was defined across all Unisys business units.

> Each of the six marketing organizations could now view marketing performance against program goals, and all six rolled up into a consolidated dashboard for CEO- and board-level communications.

> Marketers could better manage their programs on a real-time basis and make quick adjustments as needed.

> The overall business impact was observed in senior management reporting, as it provided clear, tangible evidence of the value marketing delivered.

> Marketing and sales alignment was strengthened.

> Unisys embraced more disciplined and accountable decision-making practices.

It is no surprise that Unisys has set the standard for what has become a recognized industry best practice for implementing marketing dashboards in large-scale, complex information technology companies. In October 2003, they were awarded the Diamond Award from the ITSMA for global best practices in marketing measurement.

HOW GOAL ALIGNMENT INCREASES PERFORMANCE

Goal alignment is so important that it lifts revenues and learning above and beyond the company's ability to measure short-term financial outcomes (specifically, ROMI) and long-term business drivers (such as brand equity).[2] The flowchart shown in Figure 3–1 is based on evidence from hundreds of companies. First, the use of a dashboard and consensus on which metrics are appropriate increases the company's ability to measure both brand health and financial returns. This measurement ability in turn leads to higher revenue improvement and reported learning. However, goal alignment increases revenue improvement and reported learning directly.

Key to goal alignment is to understand how your organization prospers in the short run and the long run. In his 2006 book *Marketing Champions*, Roy Young shows how to link your marketing actions to cash flows relevant to financially oriented executives.[3] Your actions build market-based assets, which in turn increase market performance and enhance the financial value of the firm. Table 3–1 gives some of Young's examples.

Figure 3–1, How Appropriate Metrics Get Results

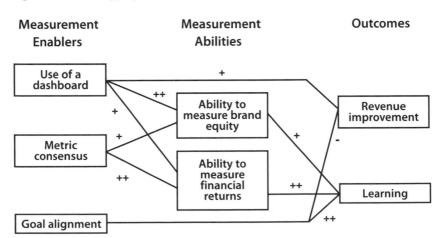

Source: Clark, Bruce H., Andrew V. Abela, and Tim Ambler, "An Information Processing Model of Marketing Performance Measurement," *Journal of Marketing Theory and Practice*, 14(3), 2006, 191–208.

Table 3–1, How Market-Based Assets Lift Market Performance and Firm's Financial Value

Market-Based Assets	Market Performance	Firm's Financial Value
Build channel relations	Faster penetration of new products	Accelerate cash flows
Build brand equity	Obtain higher price premium	Increase size of cash flows
Increase customer retention	Lower sales loss in recessions	Stabilize cash flows
Migrate to online service	Reduce service costs	Increase residual value of cash flows

In other words, what can each function do to get the firm faster, higher, and more stable cash flows? Each of these is key to investor perception of the firm, and thus its stock price.

For example, managers at mutual investment fund Vanguard know that "the *value of the brand* is astronomical compared to the value of the assets of the company" and they "measure loyalty almost at a religious level and make sure that those *measures are going the way [they] want them to go.*"[4] They go on to say: "We discuss what part of the spend we think should be measured on short-term results and what part of this do we think is image/brand oriented (assets). In our Exchange Trade Funds business we said, what would you have to believe in terms of cash flow to justify this amount of spending? And so we ran those models and said, well it's reasonable to think that if we spend this we can get this amount in cash flow and market share. And in fact we are."

Your answers to the question "what are our goals" will depend on your firm's situation and business model. For example, your company may be a small player aiming to spread the word, or a longstanding market leader that needs to look at outside opportunities in order to grow. Your business model might be:

- Testing thousands of ideas to generate a few blockbusters.

> ➤ A pyramid model of getting customers in at low prices and then upgrading them.

> ➤ An innovation leader that excels in the early phases of the product life cycle.

> ➤ An efficiency leader that excels in the later phases of the product life cycle.

For a fuller discussion of business models, see Adrian Slywotzky's *The Art of Profitability* (Business Plus, 2003).

In each case, firm goals are markedly different. For example, Payless Shoes aims to grow its customer base as its existing customers are highly profitable and satisfied, but it is not widely known. In contrast, market leader Disney aims to maximize "share of vacation dollar," which includes consumer spending on travel, amusement parks, and entertainment products. Such a broad goal helps the company identify opportunities to get more business from existing consumers.

Innovation leader 3M and efficiency leader Dell have very different goals. 3M does a great job in developing and commercializing new products, but not in defending existing products against competitors. As a result, its share of sales from new products (developed in the last five years) is a crucial success factor. In contrast, Dell offers little in terms of product innovation, but a lot in terms of channel convenience, efficiency, and prices. Finally, General Electric aims to offer new services to existing customers.

TOP-DOWN OR BOTTOM-UP DESIGN?

Let's say your dashboard vision is successfully set and aligned with your company's business and corporate strategy. Great news! However, it does not guarantee the project success or delivery of meaningful results to your company. The hardest part is not planning. It is execution. As your company moves on with a dashboard project, you will see that its outcomes and deliverables greatly depend on management and communication, to be more precise, on effectiveness of the two together.

Indeed, communication poses one of the biggest challenges for a dashboard project initiator and for its team. How can you convince top management to fully support the dashboard journey? How can you motivate other employees to use dashboards? Should you launch the project in one department, a single business unit, or in all departments at once? Look for answers to these questions in the dominant management style of your company.

Bottom-Up

If your firm has a bottom-up management approach, it will typically be the specialists, who know all the technicalities of their job, who initiate a dashboard project. As a result, it will have a very clear and specific application; however, it may lack long-term vision. Under this scenario, you would anticipate a high level of employee engagement and motivation, and rather weak support of senior management.

Top-Down

In contrast, a top-down management style typically means that a dashboard project enjoys managerial support (it is likely to be initially suggested by senior management), but it may lack employee participation. In such a case, you want to consider advantages and disadvantages of both approaches (summarized in Table 3–2) and their potential impact on your dashboard project before starting one. This knowledge will not be a universal medication for your project "illnesses," however, it will help you prepare yourself and your team for certain challenges along the way.

The Hybrid Approach

Nowadays, firms rarely apply either of the two approaches in its pure state. The two management styles can coexist and serve different needs of a firm. If a company is to make a quick decision on the operational side, it will be smart enough to use the bottom-up approach. By contrast, if a company faces an issue that has certain strategic implications

Table 3–2, Top-Down and Bottom-Up Management Designs: Pros and Cons

Approach	Top-Down	Bottom-Up
Dashboard project initiator	Top-level executives, senior managers	Lower-level managers, specialists, knowledge workers
Pros	• Broad knowledge, experience, and ability to see the big picture of the project initiators • Project aligned with the common business strategy and vision • Strategic objectives and goals are determined early in the project	• Specific knowledge of the problem and organizational needs of the project initiators • Flexibility • Highly motivated project team • Employees feel valued, as their opinions and feedback matter • Often less expensive to implement
Cons	• Lack of flexibility • Poor responsiveness • Often incurs higher implementation cost • Potential poor employee participation and motivation • Employees feel their input is not valued	• Lack of long-term vision • Inability of the project initiators to see all factors affecting the problem or company's performance • Lack of managerial support

and concerns its long-term performance, it will probably give a preference to the top-down design. Probably the best scheme to implement a dashboard project within any organization is a hybrid approach. The blend of the two management styles translates into a powerful merger of vision and strategic thinking of top managers with creativity and technical skills of lower-level managers—the perfect combination for a dashboard success!

Diageo, a leading marketer of spirits, offers a great example of a hybrid approach to goal setting. This global marketer of alcoholic beverages boasts brands such as Johnny Walker, Guinness, Captain Morgan, Baileys, and Smirnoff. The bottom-up part consists of the typical marketing plans presented by brand managers. The top-down part starts with Diageo's tracking of seventeen high performers, some within (Anheuser Busch, Heineken) and some outside the industry (L'Oreal, Procter & Gamble). Diageo aims to join the top third of this group in financial performance. Top management then considers the bottom-up marketing plans and decides which mix of marketing actions for which brands in which regions are most likely to yield the desired returns.

COMMUNICATING UPWARD: HARNESSING TOP MANAGEMENT SUPPORT

In the previous section we reviewed top-down, bottom-up, and hybrid management approaches and what impact they can have on your project. But how do you actually communicate your project scope, goals, and deliverables under different "management style" scenarios?

When management interest is not enough to make the project a success, you can work to garner management support and guidance for your dashboard project by:

- Communicating the benefits of accountability culture for your company (give specific examples—supported with numbers!—on how the company can optimize its expenditures and escalate its profits).

- Demonstrating the functionality and usefulness of a dashboard application (for this purpose you may need to build a simple dashboard or select a dashboard example available online at www.dashboardinaction.com).

- Indicating industry/market trends toward the use of a dashboard (show the statistics on dashboard adoption rate in the market, use industry or cross-industry benchmarks).

When employee interest is not enough to make the project a success, you have to aim to make the dashboard relevant to the employees' daily work lives. A good example of making the dashboard relevant to employees is provided by Discover Financial Services. This case study is based on an article by Jeff Zabin.[5]

47

DASHBOARDS EMPOWER MIDDLE MANAGEMENT
Discover Financial Services

At the time of the dashboard initiative, Discover Financial Services ranked as the third largest credit card company in the United States with more than $2.5 billion in revenues and 51 million cardholders in 2008. It also had one of the largest marketing budgets of any consumer brand, spending approximately $700 million per year on advertising and promotion.

The high level of business complexity, combined with a strong focus on business growth and performance optimization, had forced the company to become smarter and more disciplined about how it allocated assets across the business. At the highest level, Discover's marketing dashboard captured all the data that the executive team required to drive the business. Each area of the business also had its individual dashboard, which allowed executives of the various business units to understand how they were contributing financially to company performance as a whole.

The marketing dashboard put relevant data at the fingertips of the product managers as well so that they could understand the financial impact of their decisions. "It's very easy for people to get overly focused on their top-line revenue targets," says Margo Georgiadis, Discover's CMO. "What are my sales goals? What are my volume goals? How many new accounts did I bring in? But you also want them to understand: What did I do to yield? What did I do to my relative expense productivity? What's going to happen in year one versus years two, three and four? Am I going to change structurally the payback of my investment? Putting a marketing dashboard in the hands of our key business teams forces them to think much more strategically about how to drive the business further and faster."[6] Linking individual performance of each employee to the overall business accelerated dashboard adoption, improved employee motivation, and ultimately brought accountability culture to the company. As Margo Georgiadis says, "Putting marketing dashboards at people's desktops makes them smarter about how to manage the business over time."[7]

WRAP-UP AND MANAGER'S MEMO

Building a dashboard requires commitment, supported by effective communication and followed by the corporation's cultural shift toward adoption of accountability and transparency as the main pillars of business.

Its implementation is an everyday responsibility, and its success relies on the magic combination of managerial support, project goal alignment with the company's strategy and vision, and employees' engagement and motivation.

A project initiator should not forget that innovation is never easy to implement. A dashboard, like any other innovation, cannot be effective unless its users understand its functions, are convinced about its benefits, and want to use it. In other words, a dashboard should not be something imposed on a company; it should be "sold" to the company's employees in the best tradition of marketing art.

MANAGER'S MEMO

TEN TIPS ON HOW TO GET MANAGEMENT SUPPORT AND EMPLOYEE ENGAGEMENT

1. Communicate the purpose and usefulness of a dashboard for a company.

2. Explain the role of an employee in the project and his/her impact on the company's performance.

3. Emphasize benefits of a dashboard application for an employee, for example, the ability to track, adjust, and manage—and consequently improve personal performance.

4. Encourage a dashboard trial.

5. Invite employee feedback and demonstrate that it is valuable.

6. Inject a culture of accountability and facilitate the conscious choice by an employee to use a dashboard and other perform-

ance measurement tools, that is, develop a performance-related incentive scheme that will motivate an employee to keep track of his/her individual progress.

7. Incorporate a dashboard into day-to-day operations, such as at regular employee meetings.

8. Communicate the benefits of accountability culture for a company. For example, give specific examples (supported with numbers) on how the company can optimize its expenditures and escalate its profits.

9. Demonstrate functionality and usefulness of a dashboard application (for this purpose you may need to build a simple dashboard or select a dashboard example available online at www.dashboardinaction.com).

10. Indicate industry/market trends toward the use of a dashboard by showing the statistics on dashboard adoption rate in the market and using industry or cross-industry benchmarks.

CHAPTER 4

Assemble Your Team

Today's marketers must possess a hybrid of traditional marketing skills and quantitative skills—mixing both art and science. But it's not enough to have both on the team; you have to have some of each in everyone (like having a major and minor in college). We've started living this at SAP. To let the science influence the art, we gather data and feedback on our marketing ideas before we make a full commitment.

—JONATHAN BECHER, CHIEF MARKETING OFFICER, SAP

NOWADAYS, MARKETING DECISIONS ARE MADE all over a firm, depending on the nature and culture of the organization. It doesn't matter where they are made, as long as they are made well. Information technology (IT) has something to offer (data quality and consistency), as does finance (bottom-line implications) and operations (fulfillment). But so does marketing (understanding the long-term effects on customers and prospective customers and how to influence them). Therefore a joint approach is valuable and communication is essential.

Developing a dashboard requires resources from diverse skill sets, areas of competence, and levels of expertise. Choosing and pulling together these resources is a complex process that needs proper planning in the first place and effective coordination as a project moves on.

CROSS-FUNCTIONAL DEVELOPMENT TEAMS

The size and diversity of a dashboard project team vary; they depend on a project's scope and stage. One key attribute, however, is cross-functionality. A dashboard should not be left to the IT department; it should be a task of a competent and complete team. The following is a typical mix of skills and expertise required on a dashboard project team:

- Project sponsor
- Project manager
- Functional departments' experts/managers
- IT manager
- Dashboard software expert
- Business intelligence expert
- Business analyst
- Database administrator

A single individual may have two or more domains of the required expertise, especially in small and medium enterprises (a business analyst may also be a business intelligence expert, for example, or an IT manager may also be familiar with dashboard software). In large organizations, however, separate individuals or groups of individuals are likely to contribute to only one area of expertise.

First, the project manager is the glue that sticks executives, functional managers, and technical experts together. Your candidate should have strong *interpersonal* skills (team and individual leadership, oral and written communication, conflict resolution, negotiation, influencing, delegating, coaching, and mentoring), strong *effectiveness* skills (time management, decision making, and analysis), and strong *technical* skills (field expertise, industry knowledge, and project management). Furthermore, a good project manager should be persuasive, assertive, tolerant of uncertainty, open, and accessible. Large shoes to fill . . . so what are the priorities? The key to success lies in the ability of a project manager to balance "hard" project management techniques, such as schedule and risk control, with a blend of "soft" skills, such as leadership, relationship building, and conflict resolution. Effective project management means recognizing that the discipline is as much about strong leadership and team building as it is about project schedules and budgets.

The case study that follows is based on personal conversations with Paul Koulogeorge of EB Games.

CASE STUDY

NOT ALL FUN AND EB GAMES

EB Games is a global, U.S.-based computer and video games retailer. In July 2003, it had $1.4 billion in revenues but no VP of marketing, no brand positioning, and no strategic plan. Marketing received little respect and had less ability to influence its budgets. Paul Koulogeorge, the incoming CMO, set out to develop a marketing vision and strategy, take budget decisions outside of the CFO, and train and develop employees on return on marketing investment (ROMI). And he knew he needed a marketing analytics dashboard. For all this, Paul realized, he had to get four key constituents on board: the marketing department, senior management, outside video game vendors, and outside marketing vendors.

Managing downward to the marketing employees on the dashboard team, Paul assigned ROI readings and made ROMI class mandatory. He also set expectations that a marketing initiative would only be considered complete after ROMI analysis. Paul created individual development plans (some with ROMI emphasis) and shared ROMI success stories.

Managing upward to senior management, Paul set the expectation that executives would see an analysis for main marketing actions, and he used this analysis to sell a change in allocation and a dramatic budget increase. He established credibility by sharing good and bad ROMI cases, and openly discussed how to improve the situation. As a result, the CFO came to see marketing as an accountable investment.

Involving outsiders was crucial for EB Games. Video game vendors need a way to ask for incremental advertising dollars in a co-op–driven world. Accepted ROMI analyses provided them a way to do so. This two-way street built a new level of trust with vendors. Similarly, outside marketing vendors saw some contracts linked to ROMI-based bonuses (if excellent results) or discounts (if poor results). EB Games pushed the burden on their vendors to do analysis and bring value added.

The first 100 days of change already saw large benefits: each of the four constituents felt part of the process, and all accepted Paul's leadership. The company saw profitability improve as ROMI measurement and analysis insight were put into action. This disciplined thinking coupled with financial projections changed the dialogue with executives, marketing employees, and outside vendors.

TEAM MANAGEMENT IS ONGOING

Building and managing a strong team can be surprisingly tricky even to a very knowledgeable and talented manager. From project management experience, we selected five rules that help you manage an effective team.

Rule #1: Know the Stage Your Team Is In

Teams go through a number of stages after they are first pulled together, and these stages often explain why certain problems or issues arise within a team. There are five major stages that teams typically experience:

- **Stage 1:** The start is characterized by high excitement. Team members are enthusiastic, but do not have a clear understanding of their roles.

- **Stage 2:** Roles are assigned, and personalities of team members begin to show; however, some may not feel safe to be open and assertive yet. Uncertainty of team members can lead to conflicts.

> **Stage 3:** People become more confident in both themselves and their colleagues. Relationships strengthen, as differences of opinion start being respected. Goals become common and manageable—all team members are working together toward a common objective.

> **Stage 4:** Midpoint transition: similar to a mid-life crisis for individuals, teams often change working patterns halfway through the project's life. The team drops old working patterns, reengages with its supervisors and managers, and adopts new shared perspectives. Managers should be understanding during this transition, and realize dramatic progress often follows the midpoint transition.

> **Stage 5:** Teamwork becomes smooth, as team members evolve. Leadership—strengthened by careful delegation—leads to regular and effective achievement of common goals and targets.

Rule #2: Help Your Team Along in Stages 3 and 4

It is extremely important to get the "vectors" aligned in your team. A vector is a force that pulls in a certain direction and every project team member will have his or her own, created by individual principals, expectations, and values. A project manager should get every team member pulling in the same direction to achieve common project goals. The best way to do so is to create a working climate with free flow of information, regular interaction, and frequent feedback.

Rule #3: Learn What Motivates Your Team Members

It's tempting to assume everyone has the same motivations and responds to the same incentives, but these assumptions can greatly harm your team's success. Instead, take the time to learn what is most important to each colleague. Is it bringing home the bacon, that is, delivering on the essential demands of their own department? Is it a dramatic improvement in company efficiency to put on their CV for career advancement?

Rule #4: Delegate, Delegate, Delegate!

The scope of the dashboard project is huge. That's why you have brought on board several experts in their own field. Now trust them and delegate as much as you can.

Rule #5: Resolve Conflict Productively

Project teams, especially cross-functional ones, are breeding grounds for conflict. Among the issues that promote conflict are:

- **Different perspectives.** The purpose of a project team is to harness diverse skills and talents toward specific common objectives. Team members, coming from different departments or even organizations, bring different perspectives into a team. For example, in the telecom multinational Avaya, marketing and sales have very different views on the quantity and quality of sales leads brought in by marketing. Moreover, salespeople only use some of the marketing support material to close the deal. Of course, different people try to get along (we hope so ☺) but there is a tendency to stereotype and devalue others' views.
- **Role conflict.** Very often, team members are engaged in multiple roles within an organization and report to different managers, which may create conflicting loyalties.
- **Implicit power struggles.** While role conflicts typically occur horizontally (across units or departments), they can also occur vertically, as different levels of authority are represented on a single project team. Individuals, who occupy powerful positions elsewhere, can try to recreate or exercise their influence in a group.
- **Groupthink.** Team members become reluctant to examine

different perspectives, as these are seen as threats to a group's existence. As a result, they censor their personal opinions.

You can avoid many of these conflicts by building a productive and collaborative team in the first place. It's important that you select team members based on interpersonal skills, not just technical expertise, and coach them in listening, assertiveness, and conflict resolution as needed.

SUSTAINED ASSISTANCE FROM TOP MANAGEMENT

We already talked in Chapter 3 about the importance of initial top management support. In fact, research shows that C-level support is the most critical success factor for any internal or external project of a company.[1] But how do you sustain it? Dashboard project deadlines are often postponed, and almost invariably they require more resources than initially planned. When this happens—when doesn't this happen?—the issue of maintaining managerial support becomes number one on your agenda.

First, you need to find a sponsor committed to your project within the company. As one project manager explained, "a sponsor has to have the capability and the decision to influence others . . . in the sense of making sure that commitment required for resources and capabilities to implement, etc., is strong enough to make things actually happen. That's not just in the early days of the program but also to make sure that what we're trying to achieve is sustainable and it's not just something that disappears at the end of the project. So the project sponsor carries that role not just now, but ongoing for sustainability purposes."[2]

A project sponsor should be an executive-level manager, who is usually not a direct stakeholder in the implementation of the initiative, but at the same time is a very strong proponent. The best project sponsor is someone who is well respected and has political clout in the organization. A sponsor should be able to get things done when the normal channels of protocol become clogged or break down.

Besides a sponsor, the network of the dashboard project manager itself is key for sustaining managerial support for the project. You will need to continuously develop, strengthen, and further expand your networks in and outside your company, which will provide you with stronger top management support in return.

A wonderful example of how continued top management support and attention helps employees make bold decisions is provided by Progressive Direct.[3] The company is a pioneer in creative marketing actions, and they recently put in place a recommendation system that refers some prospective customers to competitors. The move generated Web traffic, which built awareness of Progressive's name, and conveyed the sense that Progressive is an honest broker. Before making such strategic decisions, however, Progressive's executives first wanted to see how the recommendation system would affect retention ratios, consumers, and distribution channels. As president Alan Bauer stated: "Give examples of how this will help the company do things faster, better, and cheaper." Bauer also suggested exploring how actions could affect competitors. "Occasionally it sent business to a competitor, which was okay. Suppose we show a competitive policy at $400 and a Progressive policy at $2,000 for the same risk, we just sent our competitor a $1,600 loss if we did our pricing right." This requires that top management have a lot of trust in the calculations—and in the employees that made the case for the recommendation system. Do your bosses have this much trust in the process?

WRAP-UP AND MANAGER'S MEMO

The major challenge for a dashboard project manager is combining the talents of diverse individuals with their different professional orientations toward a common larger task.

Effective project managers possess strong interpersonal and technical skills. These help the dashboard project team to focus on both task (timely performance with budget, concern for quality, and technical results) and relationship factors (capacity to solve conflicts, establish trust, and communication effectiveness). Barriers such as differing priorities and interests, role conflicts, and power struggles can undermine group processes and quickly derail common goals of a project team. Yet these issues are the most difficult to see and require a leader with great sensitivity to effectively confront them.

MANAGER'S MEMO

TEN KEY STEPS IN ASSEMBLING AND BUILDING AN EFFECTIVE PROJECT TEAM

1. Identify the skills needed to make your project happen, and find people with those skills.

2. Understand different stages of a team formation.

3. Create a good working climate in which a team can be productive and effective.

4. Talk to your team regularly.

5. Remember that different people have different perspectives, and adjust the way you communicate accordingly.

6. Recognize what factors motivate (and demotivate) your people.

7. Delegate, delegate, delegate!

8. Spot conflict as early as possible, and take immediate steps to resolve it.

9. Involve team members in key project decisions.

10. Keep your eye on the big picture.

CHAPTER 5

Gain IT Support on Big and Not-So-Big Data

Forrester recently called on CMOs and CIOs to collaborate more. More progressive CMOs have told us that this pairing of marketing and technology is crucial for them to build and sustain competitive advantage for the whole enterprise.

—FORRESTER RESEARCH AND HEIDRICK & STRUGGLES,
"THE EVOLVED CMO," 2012

BUSINESS AND TECHNICAL DIVISIONS HAVE RARELY BEEN the best bed partners. However, their cooperation is essential for success in marketing analytics for any size of data, just as the cooperation between marketing and finance is crucial in setting the vision, as we saw in Chapter 3. Whether you want to create a basic dashboard in Excel or invest considerable funds to purchase sophisticated real-time dashboard software, your efforts rely on technology and the IT support that comes along with it. So what are the stumbling blocks between business and technical colleagues? How do you make the two work toward a common goal?

The most common stumbling block is not involving one group at the start of the dashboard project. On one side, we see dashboards initially developed and launched by a single business unit or department without IT input. When the company later decides to scale the dashboard application, IT support becomes a must. Under this scenario IT specialists will need to adopt an original project scheme and features and adapt them to diverse functional levels of a company. That's a very big challenge! On the other side, IT is given the initial task to build a dashboard and implement it throughout a company. However technical employees rarely understand the "nuances" of dashboard users' business needs. Under such circumstances, the IT department faces a different challenge—to learn its customer!

Either way, IT and business have to adapt to make the dashboard a success. As managers, we can make this process less painful and less stressful for everyone. Let's start by understanding the different worldviews of business and IT, so we can start to bridge the gap.

IT IS FROM JUPITER, AND BUSINESS IS FROM MERCURY

IT and business appear to live in different worlds. The IT world lacks a sense of urgency that is very often driving businesspeople. Business managers are continuously under the pressure of time, competitors, and customers. Because of these pressures, the business group values flexibility and fast action. IT, however, thinks long term rather than "right now" and "today." It aims to deliver solutions that will work not only today, but that will be able to handle a higher demand of tomorrow. IT is responsible for laying a foundation that will ensure the long-term success of a system. That's why IT solutions so frequently take much longer to implement than the "down-and-dirty" ones suggested by businesspeople with a "need it now" mentality.

While the business group considers IT "uncooperative," the IT group sees most business managers as impatient and shortsighted. As the outside consultant, I see two groups of dedicated, responsible people marching to different drumbeats. Part of my job is to get them listening—even better, dancing—to the same music. And that will be a big part of your job!

Key to understanding IT's Jupiter-like world is that IT is expected to deliver a growing number of high-priority projects in an ever-shorter time period, while financial and human resources to implement such projects are continuously shrinking. In addition, their business customers are constantly adding and changing requirements. These factors very much complicate the situation and do not allow IT professionals to plan and execute projects smoothly.

The dangers of business–IT conflict are obvious: Left to their own devices, business divisions often create an expensive nonintegrated system, which will be inefficient to manage in the long run. Just the opposite will occur, however, if IT people have the key role in a project: The IT team will primarily focus on product functionality and will work hard to build a dashboard that is integrated into the architecture of a system in place, without much regard for actual use and business value.

Why is alignment of IT with business so hard to achieve? IT managers have long wanted a better alignment, but complain about the structure and decision-making processes of many modern companies. Many organizations communicate strategic objectives specific to different functional departments, directly to those departments' managers. Managers then split their objectives among their line managers. The latter do the same at departmental and team level, so that each has their own set of objectives. Eventually, these filter down to individuals, defining their specific targets, goals, and responsibilities.

This poses a problem for IT directors. Different departments request software and hardware to meet their departmental requirements, but if the individual systems are not integrated, the IT department is not supporting the whole business. Many business departments have no incentive to change the way they use technology if they feel they are already meeting their targets. IT directors, meanwhile, are under pressure from the board to ensure that systems are integrated and common technology is used. The case study that follows illustrates the need for IT–business cooperation at a multichannel retailer in the United States.

INSIDE AND OUTSIDE DATA AT A MULTICHANNEL RETAILER

At a leading fashion retailer, business and IT regularly clashed on the integration of outside data with internal records on customer transactions and loyalty programs. The retailer had excellent legacy IT systems to connect information on loyal customers to their transactions, but not to integrate this with customer online behavior and with social media conversations about the company's advertising, products, and brand. Impatient to dig into this wealth of external data, one business division quickly developed a tool on its own and started targeting customers based on the data. Unfortunately, the lack of integration ended up confusing many customers, who found themselves receiving multiple unrelated offers from other business divisions. Moreover, the new system was not very accurate in its predictions of which product a customer was going to buy next.

The retailer decided to start anew with help from IT and all key business divisions. The new system integrated online with existing data and did a much better job predicting next-to-buy products and targeting prospective customers with the right offers. The integrated databases include information on customer demographics, lifestyles, past purchases, online search history, and visits to websites of the company, its competitors, and price comparison sites. Moreover, the social media data became more accurate as it included the amount, sentiment, and context of the conversations about the company, and separated opinions of the retailer brand itself from that of its advertising and specific products.

MOVING *IT* CLOSER TO BUSINESS

The relationship between IT and business is obviously complicated. The relationship can be improved—IT and business can grow closer—but only with the cooperation of both departments and effective communication between the two.

Here are some guidelines for IT on its way to productive collaboration with business:

- **IT's objective must be to support business.** IT should recognize that its task is not to deliver technology for the sake of technology but to provide service to the internal customers of a company. To stress this point, Red Robin renamed the Chief Information Officer the "Chief of Business Transformation," which its CMO Denny Marie Post believes "is a smart move to extend the role beyond IT."[1]

- **IT must know its customer.** It is crucial that IT people understand their business clients. Reading the company's annual reports is a start, but no substitute for face-to-face contact. Sharing lunch tables, inviting businesspeople to IT meetings, and translating IT news into business opportunities are all ways to improve understanding of business needs.

- **IT must not be isolated.** Very often the IT department functions as an isolated unit within a firm. It has a different reporting structure and incentive system. It even possesses its own culture, to be more precise, subculture: jargon, dress code, and work schedule. In several of my executive education and MBA courses, IT and business managers from the same holding met for the first time! Often they express surprise learning about "the other side." However, IT should not be seen as too "separate" from the rest of the company. Technical teams that sit side by side with their business counterparts enjoy a much healthier and more productive relationship with businesspeople.

- **IT must understand the firm's business strategy.** This is vital because only with an understanding of the strategic goals can IT itself add value to the development of the tools that serve business needs.

- **IT must explain to business the IT ramifications of specific strategic objectives.** If the sales director wants to expand overseas, the IT implications of such a move (creating a shared services center, or outsourcing systems) need to be communicated. Changes to the business will have a big impact on the IT strategy and operations.

- ➢ **IT must explain the trade-offs inherent in the business strategy.** An organization may have multiple objectives, such as cutting costs, expanding overseas, and improving customer services. However, these objectives need to be prioritized, and the trade-offs that will occur as the result of prioritization need to be examined.

Further, the IT department's insistence on standardization is one of the stumbling blocks between the business and IT people. Adhering to technical standards enables the IT group to respond more quickly to routine user requests; however, very often a standardized system is not able to meet the dynamic business needs of the company's internal customers.

How can IT balance the conflicting needs for standardization versus adaptation? I recommend tools like the heat maps in Figure 1–2 (Chapter 1). Managers should obtain reasonable estimates of the additional revenues and costs of proposed adaptations, after which trade-off decisions can be made. For example, McKinsey[2] describes a fast-moving consumer goods company where IT creates such heat maps of potential sources of value creation throughout the company's full business system.

Finally, one of the effective ways to deal with the challenge of misalignment between IT and business is to create a separate business unit that sits between the two groups and is responsible for understanding business requirements of users and communicating them to the IT team in an effective and timely manner. Such business units should employ individuals who combine business skills and technical knowledge and are equally comfortable operating in either environment.

MOVING BUSINESS CLOSER TO *IT*

Business must be able to easily reshape, modify, and refine its decisions. Otherwise, it will fail to catch up with the outside world and deliver value to its consumers. In order to gain IT support and somehow secure effective cooperation, business managers should recognize how they can adapt to address sources of conflict.

- **Business must realize how it contributes to the problem.** Typically the IT group gets the lion's share of the blame for misalignment between the business and IT departments. But business shares equal responsibility for the tension. Business managers are often two steps ahead and don't allow IT people to catch up. Business focuses on immediate action and often fails to take a long-term view on a problem. Sometimes businesspeople simply need to slow down and ask themselves whether the change they are asking for is really needed. They need to learn how to prioritize and how to make effective decisions that will translate into a long-run value for a firm and its sustainable development. Business will discover that by working incrementally, it gets what it wants much faster than by trying to build a solution all at once.

- **Business must have better self-discipline.** In many companies executives threaten to outsource or offshore IT support when the department does not meet the business needs of a company or cannot cope with the demand of its internal customers in an effective manner. In this case, business typically ignores the possibility that its own decisions may have led to IT malfunctioning.

- **Business must understand how much work is involved in development.** IT managers know very well that the hardest part of a new application development is not on the surface, is not that what users can easily see. It's what lies beneath. Building and further supporting each application is an architecture that consists of hardware and software, data models and data transformation programs, metadata and security mechanisms, and much, much more. Any new application implementation requires a lot of work by IT: collecting users' requirements for a new project; building or expanding an existing data model to support the new project; analyzing and mapping the data; testing and launching the application; educating users about the new application; and more, much more.

> **Business should allow IT to standardize as well as leave room for flexibility.** We tend to want it all, right now, and for free! In the real world of data collection, analysis and storage, trade-offs and compromise are necessary.

> **Business must alert IT to changing priorities and strategies.** Just as IT must communicate the IT ramifications of new business strategies, business must communicate the business priorities. In this way, IT can plan its strategy and allocate resources.

WRAP-UP AND MANAGER'S MEMO

Business and IT have been coexisting, often in distrust, for years. The business group does not allow the IT group to prioritize, and the IT team does not adhere to priorities of the business group. The IT department must "learn its customers" and understand their business needs, and learn to think and speak in business terms. It also must develop an infrastructure that will allow it to accelerate as well as to customize its processes.

At the same time, the business needs to understand the challenges of IT support and help the IT group cope with ever-increasing demand for IT services within a company. The business group must allow IT to build a standard infrastructure that can improve both efficiency and effectiveness of the internal processes.

Business units must work with IT to transform any early successes of new applications into valuable resources of the company. Finally, both sides must recognize that there is a potential issue and each of them contributes to it. They must be aware of how much work needs to be done in order to align business and IT departments.

MANAGER'S MEMO

TEN MOVES IT AND BUSINESS SHOULD MAKE TODAY

1. IT should recognize that its purpose is to support business.

2. IT should know its customer.

3. IT should understand the business strategy.

4. IT should explain its interpretation of the strategy.

5. IT should define trade-offs inherent in the strategy.

6. Business should allow IT to standardize as well as leave room for flexibility.

7. Business should realize how it contributes to IT issues in the company.

8. Business should have better self-discipline in prioritizing projects.

9. Business should understand how much work lies underneath IT infrastructure.

10. Business should involve IT instead of isolating it.

CHAPTER 6

Build Your Database

Information is more important than intelligence.　　—JOHAN CRUYFF

*Information may be more important than intelligence, but it takes
intelligence to filter irrelevant information.*　　—NASH FRESCO

NOW THAT YOU HAVE IT'S FULL-FLEDGED SUPPORT, it's time to build your
database. Don't underestimate the time-consuming and tedious work
of cleansing, formatting, extracting, transforming, and loading
required data into a compliant database.

A dashboard's value largely depends on data it contains. In this
chapter we will focus specifically on how to develop and manage a database.

PLANNING THE RIGHT DATABASE

A customer database stores relevant information concerning a firm's
customers and contacts, and makes it available primarily to sales and
marketing people for further assessing and analyzing, in the hopes of
anticipating customers' needs. The purpose of a database is twofold: to
enable sales and marketing departments to maintain a company's current base of customers—that is, to retain them as loyal and active customers—and to broaden its base with new customers. Your company
may have a preference right now for either purpose, but both matter in
the long run.

Unfortunately, most databases do not live up to their promise. Often, contact names are kept in different places—some names are in the sales department, some in customer service, and others in technical service. Worse yet, noncustomer (prospect) information is often little more than what appears on a business card.

This is hardly an effective way to build a database, or a business. All prospecting material, including trade show literature, brochures, direct mail, and even advertisements, should encourage returns and include follow-up boxes for obtaining more information. There are lots of places to "mine" for information: sales call reports, purchased lists, direct-mail efforts, and industry directories.

When built properly, a customer database can offer many benefits to its owners. With a database you can:

- Determine each customer's value to your business.
- Identify the most profitable and least profitable customers.
- Further increase the profitability of your most profitable customers.
- Increase customer lifetime value by reducing defections, increasing the amount of money spent by customers, reducing marketing costs, and growing referrals.
- Build better relationships with your customers.
- Profile customers using a combination of behavioral, demographic, and psychographic variables.
- "Clone" your most profitable customers by searching for and identifying prospects with similar characteristics.
- Target your acquisition efforts by determining the best predictors of a profitable customer.
- Learn the reasons behind poor spending of least profitable customers and use that knowledge to increase your customers' spending.
- Model and segment customers in a variety of ways to make marketing more effective.

> Customize offers to individual clients.

> Gather information in a fast, inexpensive, and effective way.

> Determine the effectiveness of specific marketing efforts.

> Improve customers' emotional connection to your brand, product, business, etc.

In the end, a database allows you to be one step ahead of your competition through targeted communication with your customers and prospects. If you actively use the knowledge that you glean from your database, you will be able to increase sales, develop new products, and create lifetime bonds with existing and future customers.

BUILDING YOUR DATABASE IN-HOUSE

There are two ways to approach database development. You can do it yourself, in-house, or you can work with an outside agency. The first thing you need to consider is if you are ready to commit resources—financial, technological, and human—to create and maintain an in-house database.

Consider the following points if you are planning to have an in-house venture.

> **Computer system overhaul.** If your company's computer system is geared toward finance and accounting, it will take a major overhaul to tailor it to sales and marketing. It's likely that you will end up having to set up a separate, high-powered system in which marketing applications receive the first priority.

> **Data overload.** There is so much information out there that obtaining and managing it can be an overwhelming task. Emerging technologies, such as interactive networks, now disseminate more data in a shorter time than was ever thought possible. Gathering, manipulating, and managing data can become a full-time responsibility. Do you have the in-house resources to deal with this?

71

➤ **Staff overburden.** With the trend of downsizing, companies must chase prospects and satisfy customers with a lean staff. Your overstretched salespeople might not be enthusiastic about taking on research and data-gathering duties. In the long run, database and measurement systems will enable everyone to use their time more efficiently. But in the short run, there is a lot of work to be done.

If you decide that staying in-house is the best option for you, here are the four key steps for you to follow.

Step #1: Set the Objectives

The first step in building a database is to determine its primary goals and deliverables for a company. Your goals might include:

➤ Customizing promotional activities.

➤ Identifying and targeting the most promising prospective customers.

➤ Increasing adoption of a new product or service.

➤ Cross-selling to loyal customers.

➤ Developing customer loyalty programs.

This list, as you have already realized, is not exhaustive. There are as many possible objectives as there are marketing managers.

Step #2: Get the Data

A database begins with data acquisition and creation of a customer/prospect list from various sources, including internal records or historical data, often captured by accounting or operations systems.

The larger your range of products is, the more complex data you will capture to record single or bulk purchases, inquiries, refunds and cancellations, etc. These transactional demographics often represent the largest challenge in developing a marketing database for your organization, particularly if the data was captured by different agencies or stored in different databases without an overall plan.

Further, it is essential that you have authority to review all response-generating sales and marketing material before it goes to print or is populated on the Web. This allows you to maintain effective control over data that you will see tomorrow or next week. If you use external suppliers, tie in data quality to their payment. Data and database quality maintenance are very important.

Step #3: Segment Your Customers and Prospects

Segmenting your customers into various categories is the next step in building an in-house database. The most basic level of segmentation involves classifying customers/prospects by type, size, or potential. Other typical classifications include sales revenue, employees, and product purchases. A higher level of segmentation involves profiling, scoring, or modeling of customers and prospects.

Step #4: Develop Marketing, Sales, and Communication Programs

Armed with detailed customer and market analysis, the next step is execution of marketing, sales, and communication programs. Depending on your objectives, there are at least five key strategies to pursue:

1. New customer acquisition.
2. Customer penetration.
3. Customer retention or reactivation.
4. Measuring results.
5. Customer intelligence.

These steps may appear abstract before you start, but they are essential building blocks toward a usable database. The next case study shows how Inofec leveraged their in-house, highly customized database to ramp up their sales and profits.

THE RIGHT CHAIR #2
The Longest Journey Starts with the First Database Step

We met Inofec, the European office furniture supplier, in Chapter 1. The new CEO, Leon, is convinced that marketing analytics and dashboards will provide a competitive advantage. However, before advanced analytics can give him the answers to key questions, Inofec first needs to gets the right data to feed the analytics. The nature of its business presents a key problem: Due to the infrequent need for major office furniture purchases, over 70 percent of Inofec purchases are made by customers who buy only once in the two and a half years of data.

Inofec has five main sources of data:

1. A list of its previous customers and their orders, including profits and costs of goods sold.

2. Lists bought from outside vendors on prospective customers in schools, hospitals, and private firms.

3. Google Analytics information on paid search impressions and clicks.

4. Online funnel information: website visits, online information requests, and online orders.

5. Offline funnel information: customer calls to the sales force for information and orders.

Unfortunately, these information sources were not talking to each other. The same prospect could be on the list of previous customers and on a list from one or more outside vendors. Both lists had little information on the prospect's current situation or behavior. In contrast, the online tracking data was overwhelming in its sheer size. The online and offline purchase funnel were considered separately, even though Inofec employees talked about customers starting their information search online (coming to the website through paid search), and then calling up the sales force to negotiate the final price—and the sales force classified these orders as "offline." Finally, the company did not have a central database for all of its marketing actions, which included flyers (direct mail) and faxes to previous customers, purchased lists, paid search (Google AdWords), and price discounts.

To create a central database of all sources, the company hired a dedicated analyst. Based on the need for daily marketing planning, Inofec decided on daily data of marketing, aggregate customer actions (number of website visits, sales force calls, and orders), and daily profit information (profits from online and offline orders combined). With the help of three business professors, the analyst composed a dataset spanning two and a half years containing data on more than 12,000 customers on marketing activities and purchase funnel metrics across online and offline channels, making the database uniquely suited to address Inofec's management problem. Table 6–1 shows the variables in the database.

Why did they choose to measure sales in revenues? Unit sales are not informative due to vastly different prices for different furniture items (ranging from 5.50 € for a pencil holder to more than 9,000 € for a customized solution). Gross profits (profits before marketing) are the customer-individual revenues per order minus the customer-individual costs of goods sold (COGS) per order, aggregated across customers

Table 6–1, Inofec's Dataset

	Variable	How Measured?
Marketing Activity	Catalog	Daily cost of catalogs (0 on days with no catalogs sent)
	Fax	Daily cost of faxes (0 on days with no faxes sent)
	Flyers	Daily cost of flyers (0 on days with no flyers sent)
	AdWords	Daily costs of pay-per-click referrals
	Email	Daily number of net emails (sent minus bounced back)
	Discounts	Percentage of revenue given as a discount
Online Funnel	Web visits	Daily total amount of visits to the website
	Online leads	Daily requests for information received via the website
	Online quotes	Daily requests for offers received via the website
	Online orders	Daily number of orders received via the website
Offline Funnel	Offline leads	Daily requests for information received via sales reps, telephone, or mail
	Offline quotes	Daily requests for offers received via sales reps, telephone, or mail
	Offline orders	Daily number of orders received via sales reps, telephone, or mail
Performance	Sales revenues	Daily sales revenues
	(Gross) profit	Daily revenues minus cost of goods sold

for each day. A rationale for aggregating rather than considering customer-specific orders emerged from discussions of outsourced marketers with Inofec. First, Inofec's business is such that it requires an instream of new customers, for which customer-specific information is not readily available. Likewise, customer-specific data on Google AdWords click-through and early funnel metrics are not available. Finally, Inofec wanted to focus on aggregate profit effects first, in order to make overall reallocations among marketing budgets, which were readily available only at the aggregate level.

OUTSOURCING YOUR DATABASE

If you are not in a position to build an in-house database, here are a few tips on how to outsource it. Depending on your business, you may consider a data-savvy advertising agency or a direct-marketing firm. Ideally, you want to form a relationship with someone who will work with you as a marketing partner to gather information through surveys, response coupons, past consumer behavior, and lists. It's best if you can find someone who will not only implement and maintain your database, but who can also devise creative marketing strategies with long-term goals based on it.

Your marketing partner should use your database to identify ideal prospects and track industry buying habits. This information should be readily available to you whenever you need to promote a new product or cross-sell an old one.

You and your marketing partner should work together to refine your database through continued outreach. Whatever information you gather in-house, be sure to pass it along. Salespeople should regularly share information that might be useful for cross-selling and promoting new products.

Find a marketing partner that you feel comfortable with and can trust. The information you are supplying is likely to be proprietary; make sure your chosen vendor is able to protect your valuable files. The last decade saw too many cases of databases that were hacked, reducing customer trust in data integrity.

TESTING AND MANAGING YOUR DATABASE

In case you have decided to build your database in-house, you may need to test it first in order to convince management to invest in your great idea of constructing an organization-wide database. Inexpensive off-the-shelf software and hardware may help you with this task. Then, you may select an important market, baseline your current marketing programs (so you have something to compare results to), and test, test, test.

Choosing a Database

You should remember that the ideal marketing database allows a marketer to create, manage, and measure campaigns, but does not necessarily involve an (expensive) in-house programmer, even when queries become complex. As a minimum, the database must allow for the following:

- All data in one location.
- Viewed at your customer level with lifetime value reporting.
- Compatibility with your server specification and networking environment.
- Fast processing, even on large datasets.
- Real-time access from all offices and remote sites.
- A flat license fee based on number of contacts (in case you choose to use database software).
- A built-in de-duplication function when importing data.
- Point-and-click approach.
- Large suite of customizable reports.
- Extensive segmentation capabilities.

- HTML batch e-mail capability.
- Flexible security, from read-only access to full export capability.
- Facility to store Uniform Resource Identifiers (URIs) from other systems.[1]

Users Rule!

From the user's perspective, the main contact screen needs to be clearly laid out, with at-a-glance access to contact details, data protection opt-outs, and a brief profile including product types likely to be of interest, market sectors in which they operate, and whether they are an existing customer, lapsed, or a prospect. It's important to look for evidence of ongoing development. How many software updates have been released within the past two years? Is there a user group? Better still, is there a user group specifically for your market sector? If so, the system should be highly customized already and development will be ongoing.

Once again with the user in mind—a marketing database should be designed for marketers (not programmers) to use—all selections should work by a simple point-and-click mechanism.

Getting Started

Whatever database marketing road you choose—build, buy, or borrow (i.e., partner with an expert firm)—the most important thing is to get started. The most frequent reason given for not getting started is that it is too daunting and too much to handle. Just remember to take it in steps. No one has all data at once. Your first effort might be to establish a program, then put in key names, by category. It is a long road, but it will surely pay off.

Overall, keep in mind that the main goal of a marketing database is to collect, analyze, and distribute information to the right people at the right time: Information is power—but only if the right people have access to it.

Moreover, do not forget that building and managing a database should involve experimentation and innovation. Flexibility is a must, and the architecture of a database must be flexible—it must be easy to change criteria and add or subtract fields. Keep the database design simple, both in terms of architecture and resource requirements. Instead of trying to make your database do everything, focus on core functionality and determine the minimum you need to drive an increasingly personalized communication stream with your customers.

Here are some final tips on how to effectively manage your database:

- Ensure that your data is accurate and up to date.
- Distribute key information to everyone in your organization (through the dashboard).
- Develop different communication strategies to approach different stakeholders.
- Identify ineffective marketing actions and show the evidence in the database.
- Tailor your database to meet your organization's individual needs. The key to success is how well database marketing technology fits into your organization's existing structure— your people, processes, resources, and, most important of all, your mission.
- Develop a simple coding system within your database.
- Keep your database clean.
- Utilize your database at its full capacity.
- Be realistic: if you cannot get your people to enter information in a database on a regular basis, your database will not be of much use.
- Be choosy about information you track and resist going overboard: Chapter 7 and especially Chapter 8 will help you identify the most important and relevant variables.

WRAP-UP AND MANAGER'S MEMO

Ultimately, success of a database depends heavily on two factors: (1) a database must be appropriately sized and of appropriate scope, and (2) a database must be used to its fullest potential. In the absence of skill sets needed to exploit a database, it can easily turn out to be a waste of money. Remember that building a database is not an end in itself. It is what you do with your data.

The future success of your business may ride on how well you think through your database marketing. The following seven laws for "big data" are just as applicable to a database of any size.

MANAGER'S MEMO

SEVEN LAWS FOR BIG DATA

1. Maintain one copy of your data (having it in different places reduces reliability).

2. Data has value far beyond what you originally anticipate. Don't throw it away.

3. Plan for exponential growth.

4. The faster you analyze your data, the greater its predictive value.

5. Solve real business pain points with your data.

6. Combine diverse data sources for best insight.

7. Put data and humans together for most insight.

PART THREE

Design Your Marketing Analytics Dashboard

CHAPTER 7

Generate Potential Key Performance Indicators

What business questions do you need answers to, and once you have those answers what action would you take or what decision would you make? —TOM GONZALEZ, 2008

THE METRICS YOU USE ON YOUR DASHBOARD ARE CRITICAL to its value to your business. Ignoring important metrics leads to tunnel vision and bad surprises. Basing decisions on the wrong metrics can create stumbles even by generally successful companies. Starbucks and the airline and car companies I've worked with all have stumbles in their history.

So, how do you get the "right" metrics, the ones that work? I offer two stages: discovery (generating potential metrics) and confirmation (testing, selecting, and updating the metrics). In this chapter, we focus on discovery; confirmation is covered in Chapter 8.

WHAT COULD MAKE OR BREAK YOUR BUSINESS?

Where you start is important in the overwhelming realm of potential metrics offered by your colleagues, outside vendors, and competitors. Start with critical business decisions that need insights, and then work down into the data and metrics needed to support those decisions. This approach requires you to involve actual users of your dashboard, as they will determine how relevant particular data is to their decision-making process. Therefore, the first step to take on the challenging way of collecting relevant business metrics is to interview your dashboard users.

When interviewing users or stakeholders, the main goal is to identify key performance indicators (KPIs) that lead a user to a specific decision or action. Mostly the interview process revolves around three simple questions:

1. What business questions do you need to answer?
2. What action/decision will you make based on those answers?
3. Once you make a decision, what do you need to track to ensure the execution is proceeding as planned?

The first question reveals business needs and requirements of a specific dashboard user. The second question allows you to understand how deep the user wants to go in his/her analysis of a metric and what type of further analysis he/she needs in order to finally take an action or make a decision. The third question allows an understanding of what gives decision makers peace of mind and what they need to know in order to follow up on their decision.

At the level of the first question we want to determine specific data components that will compose a KPI or metric, such as measure, dimension, target, etc. The second question will help us quickly filter out the metrics and KPIs that could be considered interesting from the ones that are truly critical to the user's decision-making process. Thanks to the third question, we can provide continuity for dashboard users after a decision is made and help them adjust when and where needed.

In this metric generation phase, it's important to strive for full coverage of all factors that could make or break your business. London Business School professor Tim Ambler recommends considering these two practical questions:

1. **Do we cover each customer level?** Some managers focus only on the end consumers, others on trade partners or other types of business partners. In some industries, the opinions and actions of policymakers are important. Missing out on the perceptions and attitudes of a key stakeholder creates dangerous blind spots.

2. **Do we cover both metrics that can predict trouble and metrics that can predict success?** Many dashboards focus on the negative and raise red flags when metrics are below target. This is of course important, but may create blind spots for recognizing opportunities. For instance, a global beer manufacturer focuses its efforts too much on pushing up even minor metrics in the red on the dashboard, without delving into which metrics are performing especially well and why.

HOW TO STRUCTURE INTERVIEWS TO GENERATE KPIs AND STRUCTURE KPIs INTO GROUPS

BrightPoint Consulting developed a tool, called the KPI Wheel,[1] in order to help with the interviewing process. Since the interview is rarely a structured linear conversation, and more often is an organic free-flowing exchange of ideas and questions, the KPI Wheel allows you to have a naturally flowing conversation with the user and, at the same time, stay focused on the goal of gathering KPIs. The tool helps collect information concerning:

- Relevant business questions.
- Relevant users.
- Reasons behind importance of relevant business questions.
- Relevant data location.
- Further questions arising from a relevant metric/KPI.
- Action/decision options available based on information provided.
- Specific measure, dimension, and target of a metric/KPI.

The KPI Wheel tool (see Figure 7–1) is designed as a circle, as it embodies the concept that you can start anywhere and go everywhere, covering all relevant areas. In the course of an interview session you will want to refer to the wheel to make sure you are touching on each area. As your conversation flows you can simply jot down notes in the appropriate section, and you can make sure to follow up with more questions if some areas remain unfilled. The beauty behind this approach is that a user can start at a very strategic level, that allows seeing the big picture, or at an operational, technical, or very specific level.

Figure 7–1, The KPI Wheel

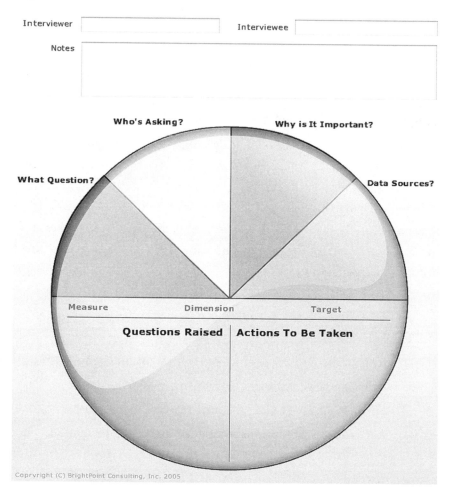

In either scenario, you are able to start at whatever point the user seems to feel most comfortable and then move around the wheel filling in the needed details.

Once you and your colleagues have interviewed your users and collected the KPI Wheels, you will want to review them together. It's best to aggregate the KPIs and create logical groupings and priorities. The case study below from an IT management firm offers an excellent example of this process.

CASE STUDY

IT FIRM GENERATES AND ORGANIZES 150+ METRICS

A major IT firm structured its KPI generation activity as I recommended and asked functional owners what three to five questions they needed answered to determine their success. This focused managers on the outputs (the "Why is it important?" question), not the inputs (e.g., the number of marketing programs on time and on budget). The process generated more than 150 metrics, coming from very different data silos such as tradeshows, customer satisfaction studies, brand tracking, CRM programs, media reports, social media, and blogs.

Next, the project team looked at the overlap between the metrics, identifying tens of metrics that were (nearly) identical in terms of the information they would provide a decision maker (the "What" and "Who" questions). The remaining 120 metrics were then clustered into twelve subcategories, and then up to four large buckets: (1) customer account information, (2) marketing performance, (3) engagement, and (4) financial metrics.

Moving on to the "Data Sources" question, the project team next investigated which types of data would be needed to feed each of the metrics, and received a first assessment of the data's validity (is it measuring what it is supposed to measure?) and accuracy (is the data clean?). This combined the "Data Sources" with the "Importance" questions, so the team could now map each metric on "metric importance" and "data integrity" dimensions. Presented with this matrix, all stakeholders quickly agreed on about fifteen metrics that were highly important and supported with highly valid and accurate data, while another fifteen were highly important but not supported with high-quality data.

The project team and senior management next decided to prioritize obtaining insights from the first fifteen metrics in the dashboard, while assigning a special team to looking for better data on the remaining fifteen metrics.

SHORTCUTS? START WITH THE COMPETITION OR WITH COMPANY OBJECTIVES

At this point, you may feel overwhelmed with the thought of interviewing all key stakeholders to obtain metrics. Aren't there any alternatives that may take less effort? Yes there are. The most common approaches are (1) checking what competitors and/or industry analysts are tracking and (2) starting from your company's stated objectives and working back to the metrics needed to track progress on these objectives. The first is called the "general approach" by London Business School professor Tim Ambler.[2] The second is known as "strategic resource mapping."

The General Approach

The general approach starts from the desire expressed by one senior executive as follows: "Keep your metrics down to a few that can be applied in every company. The metrics message will not come across unless it is simple and can be compared to other firms." Such desire is typically expressed by a firm's CEO, especially in conversations with investors and other stakeholders that love to compare the firm's current and likely future performance with competitors. Is your firm the "best in breed" on key indicators, such as the most loved brand in the category, or the most efficient supplier?

The first bucket of metrics from the general approach deal with profit and loss (P&L). It includes statement items such as top line revenues, marketing investment, and bottom-line profits. Moreover, stock market performance is important to publicly traded firms and often to the bonuses of its senior management. In my experience and in published research, stock market reaction to marketing actions may differ substantially from profit reaction to the same action. For example, costly major innovations can depress profits but be rewarded by forward-looking investors.[3] Also, some advertising campaigns may have zero impact on sales and actually depress profits, but may increase stock market performance because people like to invest in stocks of brands they know. In other words, you had better include stock price performance if it's important to at least one dashboard user.

The second bucket represents metrics in between marketing actions and hard P&L outcomes. Depending on your industry, these metrics relate to a company's reputation (often used in business-to-business settings), customer equity (often used in contractual settings such as telecom and banking), and brand equity (often used in business-to-consumer settings). Companies using reputation include FedEx and Walmart; companies using customer equity include Vodafone and Harrah's; and companies using brand equity include Coca-Cola and Procter & Gamble. Each of these approaches offers valuable insights in how your marketing actions lead to higher sales, lower costs, and higher price premium for your offers—all of which eventually increase profits and stock market performance. However, each approach also has its blind spots, which fortunately are compensated for by the other approaches.

Let's take a look at each:

1. **Reputation focuses** on general credibility and respect of multiple stakeholders (including policymakers, potential employees, etc.) and often leaves out specific customer actions, such as increasing usage and cross-buying—which is of key importance to many companies. Thus, "increased usage" is a typical blind spot of reputation approaches, but is captured by the brand equity and customer equity approaches.

2. **Customer equity** focuses on actions of current customers (including retention and usage), and often leaves out the impact of marketing actions on prospective customers and other stakeholders—which can help reduce costs, grow the customer base, and stimulate new product success. Thus, "prospects" is indicated as a typical blind spot of customer equity approaches, but is captured by the brand equity and reputation approaches.

3. **Brand equity** focuses on the halo-effect of the brand on current and prospective customers, but typically does not include specific actions such as increased usage of the brand and the willingness of current customers to accept the new brands of the company—which is key to understanding resistance to product use, for example, because of its environmental impact or because its nutritional value is suspect. Thus, "new brand trial" is a typical blind spot of brand equity approaches, but is captured by the reputation and customer equity approaches.

Start with the approach most appropriate for your industry, but add a few metrics from other approaches. For instance, brand equity metrics typically derive from a customer purchase funnel and include awareness (in different forms) and availability, customer thoughts about the brand (consideration), and customer feeling about the brand (liking). To this you can add customer behavior metrics such as trial (penetration) and repeat purchase (loyalty/retention and usage rate). Moreover, the company's reputation on the environment and social responsibility may be important in the long run, as problems in these areas can become failure causes. For example, Microsoft appeared blinded in the 1990s by its high customer equity, doing nothing to counteract its brand equity and reputation problems. Surveys showed many customers felt they had a master/slave relationship with Microsoft, and policymakers were concerned with Microsoft's near-monopoly, which could lead to excessive profits. To company managers, these concerns were unfounded: Microsoft delivered great products at very reasonable prices, and spent a lot of its profits on social programs benefiting society. However, the company did not communicate these actions to a broader audience. As a result, when Microsoft got into trouble due to antitrust cases and new competition, most of its "loyal" customers did not rally to the side of the company, but appeared to rejoice in the company's legal troubles and considered switching to the competition. Nowadays, Microsoft is tracking customer thoughts and feelings about its brand, and its reputation among other stakeholders.

Strategic Resource Mapping

In sharp contrast to the general approach, many companies like to start from their specific objectives to identify metrics by strategic resource mapping. The argument, in the words of one executive, is that: "No two companies are alike. Each has its own strategy and positioning which should determine the relevant metrics. Just as positioning requires differentiation, so their metrics should differ too."[4] We should add to that the same company sees objectives change over time; for example, priorities may differ substantially in boom versus recession times. In fact, strategic resource mapping is especially beneficial if the environment changes, performance drops, or the company's ambitions increase. The latter often happens in the form of stretch targets for subordinates.

In all these cases, strategic resource mapping helps build alignment to the key goals of the company, to compare their values to the target, and to update them when these goals change.

How does it work? You start from the specific goals for the company and its marketing department and define the metrics as what you need to track to achieve these goals. For instance, let's say this year's goal is to increase revenues by 20 percent. From your experience with the purchase funnel, you are pretty sure this requires a 30 percent increase in brand awareness, and a 10 percent increase in the conversion of leads to sales. Proposed tactics to achieve these goals include a new advertising message, a new online campaign, improvements to website functionality, and a retailer incentive program. This implies you should track metrics such as ad awareness and ad engagement, online click-throughs, website perception scores, and retailer attitudes and actions.

Where do companies get their objectives from? Diageo, a leading global marketer of spirits, offers a great example.[5] The company keeps track of seventeen high performers, some within its industry (e.g., Anheuser Busch, Heineken) and some outside its industry (e.g., L'Oreal, Procter & Gamble). Diageo aims to join the top third of this group. Top management then chooses among projects that may get them there, combining top-down (brand portfolio: which mix in which regions most likely to give desired return) with bottom-up (brand managers present their own marketing plan) to reach objectives. In other companies, top management may want to achieve market share leadership, catch up with a key competitor, expand the customer base, or maintain prices in a tough economic environment, etc.

In many ways, strategic resource mapping is the most specific approach—specific in time and relative to your targets, which may change over time. Therefore, you should always complement it with at least one other approach to include metrics of a more lasting nature.

CLARIFY FOR ALL WHAT EACH KPI MEANS

The process of gathering requirements and generating KPIs may seem like a lot of work, interrupting the already hectic day of business users. Yet, it is one of the most critical stages of the dashboard project. It's important to remind users that, if they don't give input about the relevance of metrics and data at this point, a lot more time and money is wasted. Too often, dashboard projects tread too lightly in this stage and require heavy retooling later, after the wrong dashboards have been designed, with expensive and complex data integration services around them.

The best way to avoid conflicts down the line is to obtain *agreement on key metrics used to evaluate across departments* in your organization. If marketing and finance have conflicts in your organization, pay special attention to definitions of ROI and marketing spend efficiency in terms of human resources (people per program, for example) and monetary resources (marketing communications budget as percentage of revenue, for example). If sales and marketing are key (as they are in most business-to-business companies), discuss the process of marketing handing over prospective customers (leads) to sales and the sales force's satisfaction with marketing efforts. A great example of this focus is offered by a leading global provider of business communication and collaboration systems in the case study that follows.

CASE STUDY

THE RIGHT CALL #1
What Is a Qualified Lead?

Our company is a global player in the business communications market. As typical for business-to-business marketers, its sales cycle is rather long and involves a handoff of prospects from marketing to sales departments. Both factors make it crucial to define precise metrics that can be related to the final purchase agreement. Market research revealed a huge increase in purchase probability when a prospective customer moves from the "registrant" to "qualified lead" status. Just one problem: What is a qualified lead? It turned out that the definition varied substantially across countries and departments.

Across the globe, marketers used their own definitions of this KPI, with some managers being much more liberal than others. Moreover, limited country resources and lack of perceived need for measurement drove metrics to the backseat. Allocating budgets across countries could not be data-driven in these circumstances.

Across departments, sales complained that marketing was too fast to give "lead status" to organizations that were interested but not quite ready to purchase. As a result, marketing was asked to further divide the lead into hot leads and warm leads. Further analysis showed that only the marketing hot leads and the sales leads correlated highly with near-term sales, so they should receive priority.

The dashboard continually tracks the satisfaction with and use of marketing materials by its own sales force. This provides direct feedback to the marketing department on which tools are being used and which need to be updated. In contrast to other companies I've worked with, the marketing team actually knows the sales quota and how far they are off target, so they can adjust their lead-generation activity accordingly. Joint tracking of marketing and sales metrics have made meetings much more productive at the weekly, the quarterly, and the annual level.

At weekly meetings, managers discuss new lead data, track sales and marketing performance against objectives, and suggest action when needed. Key metrics include lead acceptance percentage, funnel coverage, number of prequalified leads, number of accepted leads, ratio of marketing leads over sales wins, and revenues.

During quarterly reviews, managers add a backward analysis of sales and marketing performance, including lead acceptance/close rates. Based on this analysis, they identify funnel issues (at which point is conversion below target and what can we do about it?) and opportunities (which actions have worked exceptionally well and why?). Additional metrics include sales pipeline conversions, the ratio of leads generated versus closed, and marketing leads over win value.

Finally, annual planning cycles also consider market share, aligns sales and marketing goals with corporate objectives and market realities, and sets lead and revenue targets in joint sales and marketing sessions.

WRAP-UP AND MANAGER'S MEMO

Generating key performance indicators is an important and effortful process. Be sure to consider all plausible causes of success and failure and to interview all stakeholders on the metrics that matter to them and the data needed to measure each metric. Shortcuts include a general approach and a tailored goal-driven approach to generating metrics. In each case though, metrics should be further grouped into meaningful buckets, as illustrated by the case study "IT Firm Generates and Organizes 150+ Metrics." Potential conflict between departments should be addressed head-on at this stage, as the case study "The Right Call #1" demonstrated.

Follow the seven guidelines provided by the Manager's Memo to ensure proper coverage of the metrics you generate.

SEVEN GUIDELINES FOR GENERATING THE RIGHT METRICS

1. **Customize the metrics.** There is no "silver metric" or "silver set of metrics" that fit all firms and work for all industries. Therefore you need to create your own blend of metrics that make sense for your business and your dashboard users.

2. **Consider both absolute and relative metrics.** Your firm's sales and profits are absolute numbers, and so are many customer-level metrics, such as tradeshow referrals, website visits, qualified leads, retweets, etc. However, your performance may also be driven by relative-to-competition metrics such as relative price, relative brand liking, market share, share of advertising in your category ("share of voice"), etc. For instance, the relative quality gap and consumer perceptions of private labels (store brands) versus national brands goes a long way to explaining both store brand and national brand sales and profits.

3. **Cover all important stakeholders.** Overcome dangerous blind spots in off-the-shelf metrics by asking users about possible failure and success causes. If trade channels are key to your business, include their attitudes and actions. If policymakers can severely impact your performance, track your reputation on the key issues they care about

4. **Cover all insight levels.** Some metrics are key to diagnosing the long-term health of your company but give little insight into how to improve it. Others are much more tactical, and of more value to specific brand managers than to your CEO. This is why interviewing all user types is so important at this stage.

5. **Focus on metrics the user can control.** Some business drivers—such as business cycles, the economy, and demographic changes—are not under direct control of the decision maker. While often important to track, your focus should be on those metrics that are at least partially

under the control of the company. This is especially important if your company sets stretch targets for dashboard users, with bonuses tied to the achievement of these targets. A useful dashboard allows users to change their actions and track their progress, increasing motivation and reducing anxiety for the next performance review.

6. **Ensure data support for the metrics selected.** Information systems must be in place to provide timely, accurate data on the metrics that the firm decides to use. Without information technology, it is impossible to set up incentive systems that reward performance against the metrics.

7. **Review the metrics regularly.** In many cases, the choice of metrics depends on your company's strategy and business environment. If either changes, current metrics may no longer be relevant and should be revised. However, making too many changes is a bad sign: It's better to invest extra time up front to ensure that metrics cover the ongoing concerns of functional managers and C-level officers.

CHAPTER 8

Eliminate to Select Key Leading Performance Indicators

The art of knowing is knowing what to ignore.

—RUMI, THIRTEENTH CENTURY

Big Data is a powerful tool for inferring correlations, not a magic wand for inferring causality. —GARY MARCUS, 2013

JUST AS ANY BRAINSTORMING SESSION leads into an elimination exercise, so must your dashboard initiative turn into a selection process. In the previous steps, coverage was key: Your goal was to avoid leaving out critical success/failure factors and to elicit as many potential dashboard metrics as possible from different departments and businesses. Now is the time to narrow down that list to the metrics most likely to matter to *performance*. Most often, companies need help, drowning in the sheer number of metrics and the different opinions of key stakeholders on their favorite metrics. Recent research[1] across countries confirms performance suffers with too few (fewer than five) and too many (more than twenty) metrics. The *sweet spot* differs by country, with European managers tracking about twelve metrics, Canadian managers about eight, and U.S. managers about six. This confirms Tim Ambler's view that European managers prefer more coverage in Air Force pilot–like dashboards (ten to twenty metrics), while North Americans prefer simplicity in car-like dashboards (five to ten metrics).[2]

But *which metrics* should you prioritize on your dashboard? For internal processes, you can use several established tools in the Total Quality and Balanced Scorecard movements to select key metrics (e.g., root cause analysis).[3] Your toughest challenge will be to narrow down the myriad choices in externally focused metrics, especially regarding what (prospective) customers think, feel, and do. Examples of companies focusing on the wrong metrics abound: Continental Airlines used to focus on on-time departure, while its customers only cared about on-time arrival. Starbucks was overly concerned with bean selection and new beverages, forgetting for a while that consumers really cared about a clean store, friendly staff, and fast service. The latter insight led to the introduction of loyalty cards that sped up the long lines. At one car company I witnessed widespread panic because a so-called key performance indicator was down even while sales were up. It took a cause-and-effect analysis to demonstrate that this indicator was not so very "key," and would not lead to lower sales in the future, and that managers could celebrate instead of punish!

This chapter enables you to address the challenge of objective metric selection. First, we look at commonly used approaches and why they fail to identify leading performance indicators. Next, we propose our own method to select key leading performance indicators (KLPIs). Technically, our approach is known as vector autoregressive modeling, an econometric technique for which Chris Simms received the 2011 Nobel Prize in Economics. Through examples from several industries and brands, I demonstrate the new insights generated by this approach. The next chapters broaden this evidence by integrating new funnel metrics (online consumer behavior) in your market dashboard, and by comparing metrics in emerging versus mature markets.

Let's start by reviewing common methods in current practice, and demonstrate how we can improve the analysis and yield better insights. As shown in Table 8–1, these common methods ask customers either directly (stage 1) or indirectly (stage 2) what matters most among the attributes, benefits, and claims (typically called "the ABCs") of different competing offers.[4] We review what is wrong with stages 1 and 2 and demonstrate in case studies how stage 3 yields better metrics.

WHY NOT ASK CUSTOMERS WHAT'S IMPORTANT?

Since the dawn of marketing, managers have aimed to find out what is important to customers. There are basically two ways to do so: you can ask customers straight out (directly) or you can go about it sideways (indirectly). In this section we'll show the benefits and pitfalls of both of these methods.

Table 8–1, How to Select Performance Indicators

	Stage 1: Directly	Stage 2: Indirectly	Stage 3: KLPI
Action	Say	Imply	Do
Metric	Direct importance	Derived importance	Demand
Basis	Magnitude	Differentiation	Lead-lag time
	Frequency	Uniqueness	Dynamic explanatory power
Tools	Open-ended survey	Perceptor/assessor	Granger causality
	Closed-end survey	Conjoint analysis	Vector autoregressive modeling
Strength	Intuitive	Doesn't need customer ability and desire for telling the truth	Reveals hidden drivers of customer behavior
Weakness	Requires customer ability and desire for truthful answers	Needs statistical analysis "fooled by association"	Requires analysis of data over time
Most common metrics	Product features	Points of difference of product and brand	Communication awareness
			Imagery
			Usage occasion

The Direct Approach

The most intuitive way to rank customer-based key performance indicators is to *ask customers directly*. There are two ways to do this.

The first direct response method is the *open-ended survey*. Here, customers are asked what matters and why. Importance (of the stated attributes) is determined on the basis of "intuitive expert analysis," typically exercised by experienced market researchers who code and aggregate the data. Market researchers draw conclusions based on the frequency, sequence, and/or pattern of responses. The faster and/or more frequently a "reason why to buy" is offered, the greater its assumed importance in consumer decision making.

The primary problem of this direct approach is that consumers may lack the ability and/or desire to accurately communicate what matters to them. Lack of desire is an issue for socially sensitive and highly emotional topics, while lack of ability is an issue for ordinary purchases. Consumers may simply fail to remember that they have seen a banner ad for a low-involvement product and/or feel more comfortable stating that it was a friend's recommendation rather than a TV ad that made them try a new service. The stated impact of price is especially prone to inaccuracies. In my experience, business customers strategically overstate the importance of price (aiming to get lower prices), while consumers often understate the impact of price, especially for the purchase of new products. The second direct response method is the *closed-end survey*. In it, consumers are asked to rate, rank, or check off the ABCs that are more important to their purchases. Different from the open-ended response method, market researchers assume they already have a short list of important reasons underlying consumer preferences or choices. Now they want to understand the magnitude of their priority. Not surprisingly, like the first direct method, this approach also suffers from biases of respondents' unwillingness or inability to accurately identify what is important to them.

The Indirect Method

To overcome the direct response bias, *indirect methods* determine metric importance with statistical analyses applied to survey responses.

In the *brand attribution* approach, consumers are asked to identify the extent to which a product possesses a particular attribute, delivers an identified benefit, or is associated with a specific claim. Typically, the analytic protocol is associated with the PERCEPTOR/ASSESSOR system developed at MIT by Professor Glen Urban.[5] The importance of each ABC in "driving" behavior is determined based on the strength of its relationship with *predetermined* purchase drivers such as overall favorability, overall preference, overall liking, or purchase intent. Researchers quantify this relation through a simple cross-tabulation or, more commonly, through a regression of the mindset metric on the ABCs.

If an ABC does not differ substantially between alternative products or services, researchers conclude that the ABC is not a "driver" and, therefore, not important in establishing preferences or choices between the alternatives offered. In other words, the importance of ABCs is defined in terms of differentiation between the rated items on the ABCs.

The brand attribution method suffers from two important limitations. First, this method relies heavily on the sales conversion of the mindset metric(s) chosen. Is it preference or purchase intent, consideration or liking, that drives behavior, or some combination of both? Recent research has shown that the answers depend on the product category and the country (discussed in detail in Chapter 11). For instance, consideration is more important in driving purchases in high-involvement categories and in emerging markets, but liking is more important in low-involvement categories and in mature markets.[6] Second, the brand attribution approach ignores ABCs that show little variance across brands in the category (e.g., fast service at a quick-service restaurant). Known as "hygiene factors" or "points of parity," such attributes can still be a key driver of consumer behavior if they are (or are perceived) to be lacking for a particular brand.[7] By insisting that preference only exist in variance across brands, the attribution method favors "unique" attributes ("points of difference"). The conclusion that a particular ABC has little or no importance could either mean that all/most brands successfully deliver *or* are severely lacking in this attribute. For example, many such analyses report that "good value for money" is not important. Obviously, this conclusion is only valid in a restricted range of "good value for money," and heightened consumer price sensitivity in a recession may yield substantial behavior changes even when brands differ only slightly in "value for money."

The second indirect method is often referred to as *conjoint analysis*, asking a consumer to make choices reflecting their preferences between alternatives. No assessment of attribution, appropriateness, or belief of the attributes, benefits, or claims for the choice options is required. The research rationale is that by applying a trade-off, overall consumer preferences can be decomposed and appropriately allocated among the underlying ABCs. This partitioning process enables the development of a hierarchy of factor importance (utility) for determining the relative impact of each in driving choices between the options.

Conjoint analysis overcomes the brand attribution method's reliance on an assumed purchase driver (instead, choice is the dependent variable), but suffers from a similar focus on systematic variance among factors—the more "differentiating" the levels, and the larger the range of utilities between the levels, the more "important" is the factor.

Conjoint analysis also faces two specific issues. First, it's challenging to design a realistic choice environment with several levels of (most of) the many attributes some customers may deem important—without overwhelming or boring respondents. Second, design factors, including how choices are presented, the number of levels included, and the number of attributes shown, all have been empirically demonstrated to affect results.[8]

In sum, commonly used methods suffer from serious limitations. Of course, researchers have worked on method extensions to overcome the mentioned limitations, with some success. Moreover, combining methods helps to alleviate the "blind spots" of any one method. However, a key issue that these extensions have not addressed is the *question of causality*. By designating an ABC as important, the previous methods imply—but do not demonstrate—that significant changes in consumer awareness of, attribution to, and/or belief in that item in a choice option will in fact result in a behavioral or, at least, an attitudinal shift. Marketing priorities can then be set consistent with the discovered pattern of results.

As popularized by Levitt and Dubner's *Freakonomics* (New York: Morrow, 2009), all of the four methods can have you "fooled by association." Indeed, all four identify what is important to the consumer from data collected *at a single point in time*. Thus, all are subject to the classic statistical limitations inherent in correlation-based research and do not establish cause and effect. Ultimately, companies want to create initiatives that will move future consumer behavior, which requires an analysis of leads and lags over time (stage 3 in Table 8-1). First Tennessee Bank offers a great illustration in the case study that follows, courtesy of Dan Marks.[9]

CASE STUDY

FIRST TENNESSEE BANK TESTS ITS METRICS

In 2009 Dan Marks, CMO at First Tennessee Bank, felt that his firm's metrics were missing the mark because they were not linked tightly enough to profitability. In other words, the marketing team was spending too much time focusing on intermediate metrics that didn't really matter. Identifying the true drivers of performance required a deep analysis of more than seventy existing metrics—everything from awareness and preference to share-of-voice, number of locations, market demographics, interest rate environment, and customer service scores. Marks' team looked at three years' worth of data across five different geographic markets, running multiple regressions and fit analyses.

What did they learn? One big takeaway: Some variables were predictive of revenue, while others were simply correlated with it. For example, awareness levels rose and fell at rates similar to retention and revenue growth, but awareness was not predictive of future revenue. "We realized that while customers must be aware of our offering to buy it, just increasing awareness without providing a compelling and actionable offer wouldn't drive revenue," says Marks. "Think of Enron—they have 100 percent awareness but zero revenue." Measures more related to specific programs such as client loyalty scores, distribution changes, or even specific levels of marketing spend were more predictive of retention and revenue growth.

The analysis helped Marks's team narrow down its set of acceptable objectives, because the metrics that simply moved in sync with others were not worth what it cost to track them. Marks concluded: "We had paid attention to what we believed to be key indicators like awareness, preference, and share-of-voice. But no one had ever tested the model to determine how important they were to really drive core business performance like revenue and profit."

WHICH INDICATORS LEAD PERFORMANCE? GRANGER CAUSALITY IN ACTION

To address the challenge of predictive validity and identify metrics that lead performance, I propose two steps: (1) turning metrics into leading performance indicators (LPIs), and (2) turning them into key leading performance indicators (KLPIs). For each step, a Nobel prize–winner in Economics shows the way.

First, leading indicators are of key importance to managers: if a tracked metric changes before performance changes, managers may have time to take action and stop hard outcomes like sales or profits from slipping. The late Sir Clive Granger proposed to collect multiple measurements over time and to analyze the leads and lags in these data.[10] This "Granger causality" has been successful in fields ranging from economics to politics, and from finance to marketing. In fact, Clive told us at the 2005 Marketing Dynamics conference that he originally started with marketing, collecting price perceptions and shopper actions in front of U.K. supermarkets in the 1950s.

The principle of Granger causality is straightforward: *If a metric is leading performance, it should help to predict future performance.* In practice, the researcher compares the quality of two performance predictions: (1) based only on past performance and (2) based on past performance and the past of the metric. If the second prediction is significantly better than the first, then we conclude the metric is "Granger-causing," that is, the metric leads performance. Granger causality tests dramatically reduce the 100+ metrics generated as KPIs to only 10–20 that lead performance, as discussed in Chapter 7.

This does not mean only those metrics should be tracked; other metrics may have a diagnostic value even if they only move at the same time, or even after hard performance moves. Such diagnostic metrics can still play an important role in figuring out why hard performance has changed. It does mean that leading indicators have a value beyond diagnostics. they predict performance and are thus useful in marketing, operations, finance, and many other business functions. Therefore, they deserve priority in dashboards, which are forward-looking and help the user take action in order to increase future performance.

EB Games, presented as a case study in Chapter 4, offers a clear example of separating leading indicators from diagnostic metrics. Its analysis revealed that brand awareness, Web visits, and cost per contact were merely diagnostic. These metrics increased or decreased at the same time that performance increased or decreased. In contrast, consideration, competitive preference, inquiry, trial, and initial sales value were determined to be indicators that led revenue and profit performance in the future. Moreover, competitive position on brand attributes and customer dissatisfaction rates led performance in the long run. Sometimes, attitudes even lag sales performance. In beverages, we found that Coke Light continued to score high in brand health surveys for months after its sales were cannibalized by Coke Zero in Spain. Apparently, the guys who switched still reported positively on the brand they had been purchasing for years. Eventually, the survey answers caught up to actual behavior.

Our next case study illustrates how Granger causality easily narrows down ninety-nine KPIs to seventeen LPIs of sales revenues for the national brand and the retailer-owned private label (store brand) in a snack category.

CASE STUDY

FROM 99 METRICS TO 17 LPIs

Managers of a snack brand were worried about the rise of the private label and confused by the ninety-nine metrics outside vendors were selling to them as "key performance indicators." The product has a household penetration in the upper 90 percent range and a purchase cycle of about seven weeks. The national brand (NB) is the clear market leader, but the private label of a major retail chain (PL) was challenging this position. While prices should matter for both brands, we expected substantial differences in the predictive power of, say, awareness measures (important for the market challenger, the private label) versus, say, special usage occasions (important for the market leader, the national brand).

Our ninety-nine metrics include the absolute measures for each brand (NB and PL) and the difference (DIF) between the brands on thirty-three of those metrics. These metrics had been classified by management in seven groups: market actions, awareness, knowledge, liking, purchase intent/trial, usage occasions, and satisfaction, as seen in Table 8–2. Within each category, metrics were highly correlated, and each manager argued for their pet metric without any real evidence of its predictive value. In contrast, our Granger causality tests enabled a fast reduction of the number of candidate metrics from ninety-nine to seventeen for each brand.

As expected, we found that at least one metric out of each category matters for each brand. While price matters for both brands, the challenger (private label) should track more awareness metrics, but the market leader (national brand) should track more knowledge, liking, and satisfaction metrics. A key actionable insight emerged from the usage occasions: When more surveyed consumers wanted "an afternoon lift," "entertain friends," or "eat on the go," sales of the

Table 8–2, Leading Performance Indicators for a Snack Brand

Metric Type	Lead National Brand Sales	Lead Private Label Sales
Marketing action	Price of national brand Price of store brand	Price of national brand Price of store brand
Awareness	Unaided awareness NB	Top-of-mind awareness DIF Top-of-mind awareness NB Unaided awareness DIF Unaided awareness NB Unaided awareness PL
Knowledge	"Satisfying" NB "Tasty" DIF "Quality" DIF	"Costs more" DIF
Liking	Liking NB Feelings PL "Fun" DIF "Trust" DIF	Liking NB Feelings DIF
Purchase intent and trial	Purchase intention NB "Tried last month" NB, "Tried last quarter" DIF	"Tried last quarter" DIF
Usage occasions	"Gives me afternoon lift" DIF "To entertain friends" NB "Eat on the go" NB	"Gives me afternoon lift" PL "To entertain friends" DIF "To relax" DIF "When watching sports" DIF "When watching TV" DIF
Satisfaction	Satisfied with the national brand	Satisfied with the national brand

national brand went up at the expense of the private label. The opposite was true when more surveyed consumers wanted to eat the snack while watching TV. These results gave both brands concrete themes to promote in their communication. Finally, the Granger causality analysis showed the national brand managers they have their fate in their own hands: Their revenue is mostly driven by metrics related to their own brand. Therefore, the battle is theirs to lose. In contrast, the private label managers face a more difficult challenge: Its fortunes depend on drops in consumer satisfaction and liking for the national brand.

WHICH INDICATORS ARE KEY? VECTOR AUTOREGRESSIVE MODELING

Now that you know the LPIs, why would you also want to rank them by importance? First, you may need to further cut down from, for example, seventeen to between five and ten metrics as the focus of your dashboard. Second, the dashboard user may want to perform what-if analyses that require an estimate of the size and timing of the effect on performance when a metric changes.

Biggest Bang for Your Buck

The importance among the LPIs is assessed in vector autoregressive (VAR) models, for which Professor Chris Sims received the 2011 Nobel Prize in Economics.[11] Figure 8–1 shows how VAR models quantify dynamic effects of marketing actions through metrics, which is missing in standard marketing mix models. This makes the VAR approach ideal when you want to capture:

- ⊳ How your marketing actions affect a metric over time (marketing responsiveness).

- ⊳ How this metric converts into sales over time (sales conversion).

- ⊳ How your marketing actions have both direct and indirect sales effects.

VAR models help you explain your performance and metrics, your competitors' marketing and metrics, and even how your performance and metric use feeds back into your marketing plans. They are especially helpful when you are unsure about the exact timing of your marketing's effects on performance, about which metric is affected when and by which marketing action, about how each metric contributes to sales, etc. In fact, VAR models are designed (1) for the many possible dynamic interactions among marketing actions, metrics, and performance and (2) for calculating not just short-term, but also long-term performance effects of marketing actions and metric changes. For these

Figure 8–1, VAR Model Connecting Marketing, Attitude Metrics, and Performance

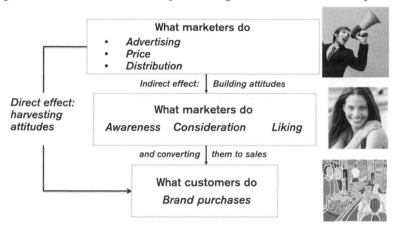

reasons, they are a most excellent engine under the hood of your dashboard.

What is the evidence? First, as you will learn in the last case study of this chapter, the VAR approach is superior in selecting dashboard metrics—compared to direct (stage 1) and indirect (stage 2) assessments and to econometric techniques of stepwise regression and variations of factor analysis. Second, as you will learn in the next chapter, the VAR approach works especially wonderfully in the new world of the connected customer, where your marketing actions (online or offline) trigger measurable consumer activity, which then translates into performance. Throughout the case studies, you will learn how companies saw substantial profit increases by acting on the recommendations derived from VAR models.

For now, we stay in the traditional world of survey metrics to provide the link between specific consumer attitudes, beliefs, and opinions and their impact as reflected in market demand data. We do so with the two managerially interesting tools derived from VARs, designed to answer the questions:

1. How much and when does an impulse (change) to a metric affect performance (impulse response function or IRF revealing the sign, size, and timing on performance)?

2. How much is our performance now explained by past changes to each variable (the "dynamic R2" obtained in forecast error variance decomposition [FEVD])?

What-If Analysis: The Impulse Response Function (IRF)

The first tool is the impulse response function (IRF); it allows us to track the performance impact of a 1-point change in a metric and/or a marketing action. For the national snack brand in this chapter's case study, Figure 8–2 shows how much and when the sales change when unaided awareness goes up by a point in week 1. The IRF figure tracks the metric's effect on sales points (Y-axis) for week 1 and later weeks (X-axis).

We learn first that little if any sales boost occurs in the week of the unaided awareness increase (week 1). Instead, the peak effect occurs on week 4, three weeks after the awareness increase. After this peak effect, it takes another four weeks for the sales impact to go down to zero. In other words, the sales response to unaided awareness shows both wear-in and wear-out: it takes three weeks before we see its peak effect on sales, and the effect lasts for about four weeks thereafter. Ultimately, sales go back to their baseline: there are no permanent effects of a one-shot jump in awareness. If the brand wants to permanently increase

Figure 8–2, Response of Sales Points to a 1-Point Increase in Unaided Awareness

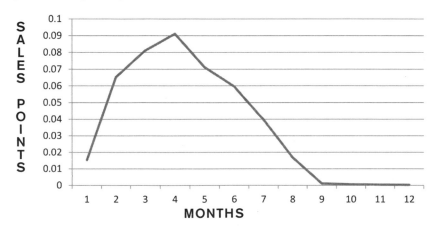

sales, it needs to keep up the awareness increase. This is typical for established brands. In contrast, emerging brands with a strong benefit advantage can see a permanent performance lift from a one-shot increase.[12]

When we sum up all the weeks in Figure 8–2, we see that a 1-point increase in unaided awareness yields 0.44 more sales points for the national brand. In contrast, a 1-point increase in liking (given aware-ness) only yields 0.31 more sales points for the national brand.

Performance Decomposition: Forecast Error Variance Decomposition (FEVD)

The second tool that has emerged from VAR analyses, the forecast error variance decomposition (FEVD), allows us to decompose current per-formance into the part that comes from its own past (called baseline or inertia) and the part that comes from each of the metrics. Like a "dynamic R2," it tells us which percentage of current performance is explained by all the past changes to each metric. For instance, Figure 8–3 shows the decomposition of the national brand sales of our snack product.

Figure 8–3, Dynamic Decomposition of National Brand Sales

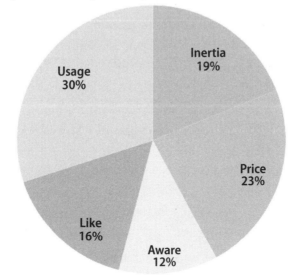

How can awareness changes have a large impact on sales (IRF in Figure 8–2) but a low importance in explaining sales (FEVD in Figure 8–3)? Because awareness did not change often, the sum of its past changes amount to less than the sum of liking, for example, which has a higher importance. We often observe this for marketing actions for a fast-moving consumer good: online actions have a higher sales impact for each dollar spent (higher ROMI) than a similar spend on TV. However, TV still drives a much larger part of the business, because managers have an easier time coming up with great TV spots than with great online actions. In our experience, the IRF and the FEVD each give an insightful answer to different but important questions:

1. If I change my marketing or a metric by 1 point, how much can I expect performance to change? This is key for what-if analyses and ROMI calculations.

2. To what extent does each marketing channel or each metric drive performance? This is key to appreciate the overall importance of a metric for driving the business.

HOW KLPIs IMPROVE INSIGHTS IN DIFFERENT INDUSTRIES

By integrating consumer responses in tracking survey data with actual brand sales provided by IRI and Nielsen, we demonstrate how to incorporate VAR modeling into a brand health monitoring program. This analysis will provide an understanding of the importance of each of the ABCs—that is, the identification and quantification of which ABCs have been driving brand sales in a substantial way, and therefore can be designated as KLPIs.

We illustrate our approach with data coming from three different industries: male shaving, food, and snacks. In Chapter 9 (on combining online and offline funnels), we will present results from fifteen more categories, including durables, business-to-business, and services. The approach is general, but the insights are often specific to an industry, so you can benchmark your analysis to the presented industry closest to yours. The data used in the first two case studies is shown in Table 8–3.

Table 8.3, Key Performance Indicators for Male Shaving and Delicacy Products

Male Shaving Product	Delicacy Product
I. Brand Presence	**I. Brand Presence**
Brand Awareness	*Brand Awareness*
Top-of-mind awareness	Top-of-mind awareness
All unaided awareness	All unaided awareness
Communication awareness	Communication awareness
II. Brand Impressions	**II. Brand Impressions**
Product/Brand Features	Core positioning "authentic"
High-quality brand	*Product/Brand Features*
Growing more popular	High-quality brand
Better shave than others	Growing more popular
Good enough shave	Has a fresh taste
Gives a close shave	Good for use anytime
Using fewer strokes	High-quality ingredients
Prevents skin irritation	Has a taste I love
Shaving against grain	Really different/unique
Technologically advanced	The best brand
	A kitchen staple
User Imagery	
Handsome	*Brand Personality Imagery*
Attractive to opposite sex	Bold
Self-absorbed	Contemporary
Ordinary	Life of the party
	Engaging
	Genuine
	Vibrant
III. Brand Consideration	**III. Brand Consideration**
Regularly/occasionally use	Regular/most often used
Purchase intent	Purchase intent
IV. Brand Attachment	**IV. Brand Attachment**
Overall liking	Overall liking
Brand I trust	Brand I trust
Brand for people like me	Favorite brand
Overall satisfaction	Relevant to you/your family
V. Brand Value	**V. Brand Value**
Good value for money	Good value for money
Worth paying more for	

In each case, the data covers the main stages of customer-based brand equity:

1. **Brand presence:** how easily the brand comes to mind. This is measured as top-of-mind awareness (the brand comes to mind first when a consumer thinks about the category), all unaided awareness (the brand is mentioned by the consumer at all), and communication awareness (the consumer remembers having seen any brand communication—advertising, promotion, etc.—in the last six months)

2. **Brand impressions:** what the consumer thinks about the brand's key features or attributes and how the consumer feels about the brand. The exact questions differ by category. The male shaving product could make you feel "handsome," the delicacy can make you feel like "the life of the party."

3. **Brand consideration:** how many consumers consider your brand and intend to buy it?

4. **Brand attachment:** how satisfied and loyal are your brand's consumers?

5. **Value for money:** do your brand's benefits justify its price?

When possible, our comparison in the case studies is with the (1) brand ratings data typical for PERCEPTOR/ASSESSOR-based systems and (2) reduction techniques such as stepwise regression and reduced rank regression (an appropriate variation on factor analysis). As to PERCEPTOR/ASSESSOR, this MIT-developed system has been tested for over 3,000 new fast-moving consumer goods.[13] To assess the technique, we regress three common and frequently used dependent variables (purchase intent, overall liking, and overall satisfaction) on the KPIs. As to stepwise regression, this technique is often used in practice to select KPIs among many alternatives.

Shave Down to the KLPIs

For a male shaving product, consumers were segmented and asked to rate ABCs in a one-shot segmentation study (direct method), and followed over two years in a brand-tracking study.

In the segmentation study, consumers were asked directly to rate the ABCs in Table 8–3, column 1 (direct importance rating). Seven ABCs, pre-identified by the client as key metrics, were included in both the segmentation and the tracking study. In the brand tracking study, ratings of brands on ABCs were analyzed using both our VAR method to identify performance indicators that lead and are most important (KLPIs) and the indirect method of "derived importance analysis," which regresses three dependent variables (purchase intent, overall liking, and overall satisfaction) on the brand metrics.

Which type of metrics do you believe came out on top? Our approach (based on what consumers do) yields different results than the direct importance rating (based on what consumers say), and the indirect assessment (derived importance) ratings (based on what consumers *imply*).

First, communication awareness leads sales and has about *ten times* the sales impact of any other KPIs in the VAR analysis, clearly qualifying it as a KLPI. The VAR model also demonstrates that the KPIs "allows shaving against the grain" (product feature) and "good enough shave" (satisfaction metric) are the strongest product/brand KLPI sales drivers. Similarly, being portrayed as "ordinary" (not a beauty model), but still "attractive to the opposite sex," and not "self-absorbed" are the strongest KLPI user images. Based on our analysis, brand managers choose these imagery elements to be part of the brand's future copy platform. In contrast to our finding of *sales* drivers, the derived importance analysis does not detect a significant effect of communication awareness on purchase intent, overall liking, or overall satisfaction. Also, "good enough shave" and "allows shaving against the grain," both of which show a strong sales impact in the VAR analysis, do not emerge as significantly stronger than the other product/brand features in the derived importance analysis. As managers came to realize, consumers do not always tell you what they are going to do. Communication awareness and "good enough" perceptions are strong drivers of sales, but fail to show up when asking consumers about liking and purchase intent.

How did the brand's "key positioning" differentiators hold up to scrutiny? First, "gives a close shave" is rated higher than any other KPI in the direct importance rating, but fails to show up in derived importance analysis or in the VAR analysis. This surprised the engineers, who believed that "close shave" perceptions were a key driver of sales. In contrast, the KPI "is technologically advanced" was the least important KPI in direct importance ratings, but is found to be a KLPI in the VAR analysis. This technology claim was considered by marketing to be important in the brand's positioning. The confirmation of this intuition led management to prefer "technologically advanced" over "gives a close shave" as a focus for future campaigns.

Finally, there was also some agreement between the VAR results and the derived and direct importance ratings. Both the KPI "worth paying more for" (brand value) and "allows shaving against the grain" (brand impression) came out on top in any method.

Delicious in a Few KLPI Bites

In column 2 of Table 8-3, you find the metrics for a delicacy product, based on two years of survey data. This brand is highly differentiated in its category and strongly positioned on the "authentic" attribute. Unlike in the male shaving analysis, a large number of KPIs qualify in the VAR analysis as KLPIs. In fact, every group of metrics is represented, as at least one KPI from each group qualifies as a KLPI. For brand presence, all three metrics are KLPIs: top-of-mind awareness has a stronger impact than all unaided awareness, and communication awareness has its own separate impact. As for brand features, "has a fresh taste," "really different/unique," and "a kitchen staple" had a higher sales impact than "authentic" and "the best brand." All imagery variables mattered, with "engaging" and "contemporary" having the largest sales effect. "Regular" consideration, liking, and "favorite brand" mattered, as did "good value for the money."

Comparing the VAR results with the derived importance measures shows that many KPIs are recognized to be important in both analyses. Still, differences abound. First, communication awareness, the core positioning for the brand, and nearly all of the user images have derived importance scores much lower than the other metrics, even though the VAR analysis demonstrates that all of these metrics had a large impact on sales. In fact, communication awareness is among the strongest of the KLPIs. Also, the brand personality imagery was hardly picked up by the derived importance scores. However, in the VAR analysis, two brand personality images, "contemporary" and "engaging," generate more sales than any product/brand feature other than "a kitchen staple."

Of the three dependent variables in the derived analysis (liking, purchase intent, and overall satisfaction), only liking also makes a strong contribution to sales in the VAR analysis. This is a key problem for derived importance analysis: Because of the high correlation between the three dependent variables for this delicacy product, two of its three regressions are redundant.

As a result of this analysis, managers decided to focus on increasing (and maintaining) liking and communication awareness by focusing campaigns on the theme of "contemporary kitchen staple that engages you by its unique fresh taste."

Across the male shaving and the delicacy cases, you see that the VAR analysis identifies communication awareness and several emotional buying factors as KLPIs, and that many of these are missed by other approaches. But does that mean the VAR-selected metrics are more predictive than the metrics suggested by other analytic approaches? Let's analyze this in the next section.

Snack KLPIs: The Power of Prediction

Remember the leading national brand of snacks from the case study earlier in this chapter? Thanks to Granger causality tests, ninety-nine KPIs were reduced to the seventeen KLPIs you saw back in Table 8–2.

Starting from those, how can different econometric methods further reduce it to, let's say, ten metrics? The company chose ten as a compromise between the five to ten metrics preferred by U.S. managers versus the ten to fifteen preferred by their European counterparts.

The VAR method was compared with stepwise regression (a popular technique that includes/excludes variables based on how much they add to sales explanation) and reduced rank regression (a factor analysis method that groups metrics by their power to explain sales). The methods were compared based on two criteria:

1. How much do they explain sales in the analyzed data period (in-sample explanation)?

2. How well do the selected metrics predict sales in the future (out-of-sample prediction)?

The results are easy to interpret, as they all fall between 0 (no error) and 1 (all error).[14]

All three methods perform rather well in-sample and out-of-sample because they were fed only with leading performance indicators to begin with. However, Figure 8–4 shows the interesting contrast between each method's errors in explaining sales in-sample versus forecasting sales out-of-sample.

Figure 8–4, VAR Has the Lowest Forecast Error

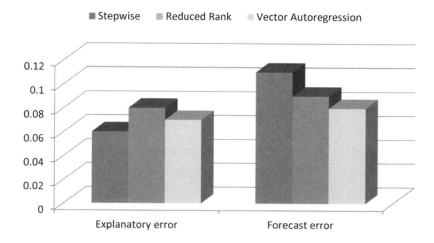

Stepwise regression performs best in-sample, but worst out-of-sample. We observe the same pattern for our analysis of the store brand. This demonstrates that stepwise regression (also called "unwise regression" by UCLA professor Ed Leamer) is simply curve fitting within the analyzed period, which generally hurts for future prediction.[15]

Reduced rank analysis (and other methods based on factor analysis) performs worst in-sample, but better out-of-sample compared to stepwise regression. Unfortunately, it's rather cumbersome to implement compared to both other approaches.

Finally, the proposed VAR method performs best out-of-sample. The improvement in forecasting error is 16 percent moving from stepwise to reduced-rank regression and 7 percent moving from reduced-rank regression to VAR. For the store brand (not shown here), the improvement is 12 percent moving from reduced-rank regression to VAR.

In sum, the best forecasting performance results from the set of metrics selected by VAR. Why is this the case? VAR is the only method to account for dynamic interactions among candidate metrics in calculating how much they explain the dynamic variation in performance.[16]

When does each metric yield its peak impact on sales? Table 8–4 shows the size and timing of the impact of each selected dashboard metric on national brand sales.

For short-term (same-week) effects, both the sign and the relative magnitude of the effects are in line with management expectations: its price has the largest immediate impact on sales, followed by the store brand's price. In the long run, however, the store brand's price has a larger effect on national brand sales than the national brand's own price! This reversal is driven by both the post-promotion dips after national brand price discounts and by the slow decay of the harm that store brand price cuts inflict on national brand sales. The likely reason is increased consumer price sensitivity, which hurts long-term sales of the more expensive brand. As a result, national brand managers are correct to worry about the growth of store brands, and they have a very limited ability to turn the situation around with price changes.

Table 8–4, Size and Timing of Each Dashboard Metric's Effect on National Brand Sales

	Short-term	Long-term	Wear-in*	Wear-out*
Price of national brand	−161,794	−84,417	0	8
Price of store brand	71,561	121,997	0	1
"Gives me afternoon lift" NB	32,129	32,129	0	0
"Trust" DIF	23,707	23,700	0	0
"Quality" DIF	0	66,963	1	0
Liking NB	0	40,420	1	0
"Tried last month" NB	0	72,481	2	4
"To entertain friends" NB	0	60,071	2	3
Satisfied with the national brand	0	46,788	2	0
Unaided awareness NB	34,164	68,537	3	4

"Wear-in" is the number of weeks it takes until the peak sales impact is reached (with 0 meaning the peak impact is immediate), and "wear-out" is the number of weeks with significant effects after peak impact. The variables are ordered first by impact wear-in time, then by impact size (absolute value).

In contrast, the large effects of the other metrics point to several levers national brand managers can pull. First, the national brand derives a strong immediate benefit from its trust gap with the store brand and from national brand usage as an afternoon lift. The immediate effect of these survey metrics is only two to three times smaller than the competitive price effects and may be influenced directly by national brand marketing communication. After one week's delay, the quality difference between the national brand and store brand is important, followed by the metric "liking if tried the national brand." Thus, the national brand's excellent quality and consumers' brand perceptions associated with the brand are main weapons in the battle with store brands, consistent with recent discussions in literature.

After two weeks' delay, the metrics "tried the national brand in the last four weeks," "national brand usage to entertain friends," and "national brand is satisfying" become important. Free samples and other trial inducements may complement marketing communication focusing on how perfect the national brand is for entertaining friends and how satisfying it is to eat. Priming consumers to consume the product in public benefits the national brand, consistent with its dominance in usage occasions with a higher social expressive or sign value. Finally, the importance of unaided awareness, at three weeks' delay, suggests that even popular brands still must ensure that the brand name comes to mind first when the consumer is thinking about the product category.

In sum, national brand managers found the VAR-based findings to be actionable. For the national brand, nine out of ten metrics were to some extent under managerial control (with store brand price being the only exception). Insights on the timing of each effect and the size of short-term and long-term impact helped managers develop better marketing plans. In Chapter 13, you will see how a company saw a fourteen-fold profit increase from acting on VAR-based results.

WRAP-UP AND MANAGER'S MEMO

In this chapter, you learned how a combination of Granger causality tests (identifying LPIs) and VAR models (identifying the KLPIs) generates a manageable list of metrics that are leading indicators of brand performance. Across several different industries, our approach has shown that these metrics are indeed often KLPIs and have a greater impact on brand sales than product/features-based KPIs. In essence, by focusing on dynamics rather than relying on data from a single point in time, the VAR approach helps you to avoid being "fooled by association."

We shared multiple examples from ongoing brand health tracking programs, demonstrating how VAR models, when applied to brand health metrics and sales data, can identify those consumer metrics that have the greatest impact on in-market sales/share. More specifically, the VAR analytic protocol presents an approach for qualifying KPIs as KLPIs and quantifying the sales impact of each KLPI.

MANAGER'S MEMO

THREE THINGS TO REMEMBER ABOUT KLPIs

1. Communication awareness and emotional factors play a key role in the consumer choice process. Vector autoregressive modeling captures these roles, while traditional importance assessment systems often don't.

2. The availability of VAR-derived information enables marketers to focus marketing initiatives on those KLPIs expected to have a meaningful sales impact. I show in later chapters that allocating marketing efforts among those KLPIs increases return on marketing investment.

3. Beyond your own marketing, the VAR approach easily incorporates short-term and long-term effects of competition. This can help you to identify points of difference and points of parity with competition, so you can further differentiate your offer on dimensions important to customers.

CHAPTER 9

Include Emerging Channels: KLPIs for Online and Social Media

We did a wonderful . . . commercial on the Super Bowl . . . for Mitsubishi Gallant . . . that stops at the end and [says] go to seewhathappens.com. We got about 600,000 clicks. Was that great or was that not great? We told the client it was great, so it was great [nervous laughter from the audience of advertising agencies].

—DONNY DEUTSCH

THE INTERNET REPRESENTS THE NEW FRONTIER in metrics. On the one hand, the online medium got big by promising advertisers better accountability and actionable insights. Web 2.0 and social media added the excitement of tracking and influencing consumer-to-consumer conversations. The current hype involves the "big data" gold mine of online behavior metrics. On the other hand, extracting this gold has never appeared more daunting. Online managers feel overwhelmed and are torn in different directions. The "next big thing" of the year (or month) ends up complicating instead of simplifying the vast array of online options—let alone their comparison with offline alternatives to allocate limited marketing budgets. As Jonathan Becher, CMO of SAP, recalls[1]:

A CMO of a large company told me she was thrilled that her team tweeted 1.2 million times in 2012—surpassing its goal of 1 million. These kinds of "ego metrics"—website page views, Facebook fans, conference attendees, etc.—look great on a dashboard but don't really move the needle for the business. I believe we should track outcome metrics, not activities. For example, instead of asking how conference attendees rate a session, how about analyzing which sessions correlated with attendees who later bought something? Ultimately, the CMO I was talking to decided that a better metric would be the percentage of non-employee followers who re-tweeted the company's tweets—a measure that would provide insight into how the market was amplifying the company's message.

In sum, advocates for emerging channels often claim that, because the medium is unique and different, the metrics should also be unique and different. This is not the case: You should aim to capture how you "move the needle for the business" for every channel that eats up a considerable amount of your money and/or time. To gain insights into which metrics to put on your dashboards, we need to examine how online and social media are different from—and how they are similar to—traditional media.

WHAT IS TRULY DIFFERENT ONLINE?

The bubble-bust-integration cycle in Figure 9–1 is key to putting new media into perspective. When radio first appeared, it was claimed that it would completely replace the written word in advertising. The same assertion was made for TV and more recently for online marketing. Inflated expectations give rise to a financial bubble, which turns into a bust and is followed by disillusionment. Based on the work by economist Carlota Perez,[2] the Gartner Group developed its "Hype Cycle" graph, in which disillusionment is followed by a period of enlightenment, which is in turn followed by productivity.[3] In the end, the new media finds its proper place in the arsenal of weapons at the marketer's disposal.

Online display ads offer an interesting case study in the typical

Figure 9–1, Hype Cycle of Emerging Technologies

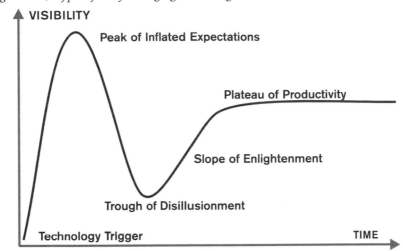

dynamics of online marketing tools. At first, online display was herald-ed as the best new way to advertise; not only can you target ads to the right prospect at the right time (when she is looking at related content), but you only pay for those prospects who click through to your website. Why would you ever pay for impressions (gross rating points) of "old-time" media such as TV, radio, and print? Then the display ad bubble turned to bust. Display ad click-through rates fell (from 78 percent on the first banner ads on HotWired in 1994) to less than 0.1 percent in 2013. Moreover, a 2012 study from the startup Pretarget and ComScore revealed that "even when a user clicks on an ad, the correlation between that click and a conversion is virtually nonexistent."[4] In response, the online display industry now proclaims click-through is not necessary for impact, and ironically requests to be evaluated by "old time" media metrics such as increased awareness by exposure and how online display increases the conversion of later marketing actions, such as search. Indeed, research just completed by Harvard Business School professor Sunil Gupta, together with Pavel Kireyev and myself, shows that online display for a bank increases the sales conversion of online search.[5] In the end, online display becomes one of the weapons in the marketer's arsenal, judged by its effectiveness in moving customers through the purchase funnel/decision journey and by its efficiency (return on investment) in doing so. This integration gives the best chances for actual productivity of the display ad technology. From this integrated perspective, much of what we learned in Chapter 8 can be applied directly to measuring online exposure.

What is truly different online? First, many online advertising forms do not simply work through exposure; they require a deliberate customer action. Second, *social media* involves (prospective) customers talking to each other, sharing both positive and negative stories. Companies have a unique opportunity to host, track, influence, and join these conversations. Third, it's very easy and inexpensive to experiment with ad executions online. Like a multi-armed bandit from probability theory, you can play dozens of "slot machines" of slightly tweaked messages and observe in real time which one is working out best; naturally you will put most of your money on the winning executions.

CUSTOMER-INITIATED CONTACT METRICS

Many online advertising forms do not simply work through exposure; they require a deliberate customer action. Current examples of such customer-initiated contacts (CICs) include search (organic and paid), price comparison sites, referrals, and retargeting (which is triggered by the customer having visited the company's website). Because CICs require (some form of) consumer interest, increases in these activities should have a higher sales effect than firm-initiated contacts (FICs) have. Indeed, empirical studies report that CICs have a much higher sales elasticity (percentage increase in sales from a 1 percent increase in marketing spending).

Classification of CICs

CICs are further classified as "content-separated" activities and "content-integrated" activities in my recent paper with Evert de Haan and Thorsten Wiesel.[6] We define "content-integrated" marketing communications as advertising or other promotional (paid or unpaid) activities on third-party websites that are an integral part of the medium's editorial content. For instance, consumers specifically access price comparison sites or organic search sites to obtain information on the searched-for items. In contrast, "content-separated" advertising means that the information, message, or offering of the advertisement is not part of the editorial content of the medium. Retargeting messages and paid search advertising (typically appearing at the right, top, or bottom of the loaded site) are examples of content-separated activities. Table 9–1 compares the "firm-initiated versus customer-initiated" dimension with the "content-separated versus content-integrated" dimension.

Table 9–1, Classification of Communication Media

	Firm-Initiated	Consumer-Initiated
Content-separated	TV ads Radio ads Emails	Search engine advertising Retargeting
Content-integrated	Product placement Editorials Public relations	Affiliates Portals Price comparison Referrals

Content-Integrated Customer-Initiated Contacts

Content-integrated customer-initiated contacts (CICICs) should have the highest sales impact for two reasons. First, prospective customers are more attentive to information that is directly relevant to what they are looking for, while firm-initiated advertising often reaches them at the wrong time and with a suboptimal message. Second, content-integrated FICs, such as product placement, are found to be more informative and more amusing, but less irritating than content-separated activities.

Interestingly, content-integrated and content-separated CICs are equally able to attract people to your homepage. However, content-integrated CICs are much better in attracting people to the next stages in the funnel. Last-click attribution methods do not account for this power and thus highly underestimate the importance of content-integrated CICs. Last click only tracks through which activity a customer came (directly) to the website, neglecting brand exposure. For the retailer studied by de Haan, Wiesel, and myself, switching from the current allocation to the last-click method would decrease revenues by 28 percent, while the retailer would increase revenue by 17 percent when following the KLPI method. This result is driven by reallocating marketing budgets to content-integrated CICs such as comparison sites and portals.

Why Last-Click Attribution Methods Are Wrong

If tracking the full customer conversion has such large benefits, why are many managers still using last-click attribution methods, which give credit to the last channel that the website visitor touched? First, they may believe that last-click attribution, or its recent more sophisticated versions, are not that far off the mark. Second, they may not be responsible for what happens after the prospective customer reaches the website. Last-click attribution does an especially poor job in distinguishing between clicks that lead to conversion and clicks that don't. Moreover, last-click attribution favors marketing channels at the end of the purchase funnel (paid search) at the expense of earlier exposure at the top of the purchase funnel (banner ads). A final reason for the use of a last-click attribution method is that managers feel there is no better alternative that is easy to implement. My experience shows otherwise: multichannel attribution studies take only a few weeks to execute and pay back for their cost within months, thanks to the much better decisions the company can make.

Instead of adding this year's new CICs and studying them in isolation (as typical in last-click attribution methods), the savvy manager will consider how and where the advertised product can be integrated in the content of the media the prospective customer interacts with. This could not only be the case for online forms of advertising, but also for more traditional forms of advertising and other firm- or customer-initiated contacts. Editorials, product placements, and public relations are appealing options. This will increase the amount of "neutral" brand contacts that customers have, and could positively influence brand awareness and brand perception. Managers can address the declining effectiveness of advertising by finding better ways of integrating commercial messages in information that customers themselves are searching for.

CAPTURING CONVERSATION TOPIC DYNAMICS IN SOCIAL MEDIA

Coke's CMO Joe Tripodi describes why the company is shifting from measuring *impressions to expressions*:[7]

> . . . Consumers have become empowered to create their own content about our brands and share it throughout their networks and beyond. It has changed my role as the CMO as we work to double business by 2020.

> In the near term, "consumer impressions" will remain the backbone of our measurement because it is the metric universally used to compare audiences across nearly all types of media. . .

> In addition, we are increasingly tracking "consumer expressions. To us, an expression is any level of engagement with our brand content by a consumer or constituent. It could be a comment, a "like," uploading a photo or video or passing content onto their networks. . .

Tripodi then goes on to propose the following keys to success in social media:

- ➤ Accept that customers can generate more messages than you ever could.
- ➤ Develop content that is "liquid and linked."
- ➤ Accept that you don't own your brands; your consumers do.

> Build a process to share success and failure quickly throughout your company.

> Be a facilitator who manages communities, not a director who tries to control them.

> Speak up to set the record straight, but give your fans a chance to do so first.

Indeed, success in social media requires a lot of creativity and experimentation, together with rigorous and real-time measurement to spot success and failure. I like to compare a company's management of social media to driving in Istanbul, my new hometown:

1. **Lanes are optional.** Customers jump from platform to platform so you should not have silos either. Istanbul traffic police do not sanction moves that make the traffic flow smoother.

2. **Priority rules are optional.** You can't depend on stable rules about customer engagement. Instead, you need to be fully alert to subtle changes and react to them fast and appropriately. Automatic pilot and distractions are what gets you in trouble. Istanbul traffic police will ticket you for talking on your cell phone.

3. **Red lights are essential.** You need to decide on key metrics that precede any major social media disaster. Everyone in the organization respects the red flags these metrics raise, just as cars actually stop for red lights in Istanbul.

Together, these rules for social media management aim to strike the delicate balance between letting go (as social media gurus tell us to do) and staying on top of things (as our bosses want us to do) — "organized chaos" at its best.

A great example of all three rules is provided by Avaya. With its roots going back over a century, from AT&T to Lucent Technologies, Avaya is a global provider of contact centers, networking, unified communications, and video products in more than 140 countries. How does a business-to-business company effectively integrate online chatter into its metrics and take action? Avaya listens in social media to uncover qualified sales leads and plugs them into existing lead-nurturing processes.[8] Sometimes the demand is explicit and classified as a "hot lead," sometimes it requires further probing as a "warm lead." For example, a tweet like "time for a new phone system very soon" obtained a response "let me know if we can help" within minutes, and led to a $250,000 contract within weeks. When the expressed need is less immediate, the "warm lead" is nurtured with both traditional and digital content tools to move it along the purchase funnel.

Despite considerable disagreement over the need for outcomes-based metrics, managers I've talked to agree on the following three rules for social media marketing:

1. Begin with setting clear marketing goals and objectives and then move on to metrics.
2. Use both quantitative and qualitative metrics—there is no "silver bullet" metric.
3. Use metrics specific to your company, business, and marketing goals and objectives.

However, most companies sin against these rules, focusing on the "easy" quantity metrics provided by the popular platforms such as Facebook, LinkedIn, and Twitter. Recent research has shown it is important to track the following four kinds of metrics: quantity, sentiment, dispersion, and topic.[9]

Quantity (or *volume*) metrics include Facebook "likes" and "talked abouts," Twitter and LinkedIn "followers," etc.

Sentiment metrics distinguish how many of the social media mentions are positive, negative, or neutral.

Dispersion metrics show how much social media mentions differ in their sentiment. For example, the wildly successful book *Fifty Shades of Grey* gets mostly five-star or one-star reviews.

Finally, *topic* metrics give insights into what people are talking about. For example, the initial social media for the first iPad consisted of thousands of online mentions, with the breakdown shown in Figure 9–2.

How Dispersion Affects Your Performance

The value of quantity and sentiment appears rather obvious, and several studies have shown their separate impact on sales outcomes, so we'll leap ahead to *dispersion*. Dispersion of sentiment, ratings, etc., is a fascinating metric, which affects the dynamics of your social media performance. Recent research has shown perverse dynamics in electronic word of mouth (WOM).[10] When initial product ratings are consistently positive (low dispersion), highly involved customers feel motivated to stand out and share only lower ratings. After all, why spend the time adding a glowing review to a consistent and long list of glowing reviews? This is bad news for the product supplier, who sees ratings drop over time. Less-than-fair ratings hurt customer acquisition, but may also hurt customer retention to the extent WOM influences the satisfaction a user gets from experiencing the product.

How can firms manage this *process*? In two ways. First, companies

Figure 9–2, Apple iPad Online Mentions, by Sentiment and Conversation Topic

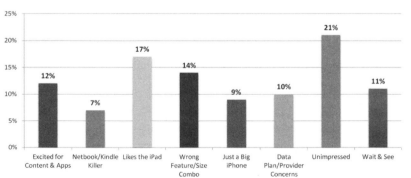

need to engage the less-involved (happy) customers to post reviews. Second, companies should enable highly involved customers to stand out without posting negative reviews, for instance by including them in new product development to improve on current product weaknesses.

The Importance of Topic

As for *topic*, it's crucial to know exactly *what* people are talking about. For example, Apple's first iPad got 54 percent negative mentions in the first months, but many of those related to the data plan or service provider, not to the device itself. On the positive side, social media data provider Crimson-Hexagon distinguishes "I love the brand" from "I love their ads." Likewise, the majority of social media mentions on a brand are typically classified as "neutral," such as "I just went there," "we bought it," etc. A recent study shows that such "neutral" conversations, contrary to what you might have expected, can have a huge impact on future sales. After all, WOM is not just following what people say, but also what they do. Social media KPI and dashboard providers such as Buzzrank and SDL show both quantitative metrics, such as positive and negative mentions, and the exact wording of the top tweets and Facebook posts, adding quality and deeper insight to quantity.

Linking Social Media to Sales and Profits

Of course, social media KPIs need to be linked to sales and profit outcomes, just as other performance indicators that are shown to lead performance and are most important to it (KLPIs). As expressed by one manager: "Last time I checked, no CEO wakes up in the middle of the night and says, 'I need more likes, retweets, higher sentiment, more open rates, or even more Marketing Qualified Leads.'"

Some social media experts claim that aiming for ROMI measurement is infeasible or even counterproductive. I disagree. Whenever companies make substantial (monetary or time) investments in social media, they should project and measure the monetary benefits. Yes, social media is not about push or control but about conversation and influence. The same goes for the benefits of sponsorship, traditionally tough to measure—but it can be done and has been done.

How? The company builds a database over time of all factors that may impact sales, and then isolates the separate impact of each marketing activity, including social media. This does require some experimentation in your marketing plan. For example, if you always include the same level of social media activity with a TV campaign, you cannot separate the sales effects. Some companies use controlled field experiments in which social media efforts are switched off under specific conditions. If you can't do that, try to double or halve the social media efforts on a specific project. The results will give you enough change in your data to analyze the impact of social media, and run more informed experiments later.

CASE STUDY

FASHION RETAILER ANALYZES THE EFFECTS OF SOCIAL MEDIA

In 2012, the Marketing Productivity Group (www.mproductivity.com) analyzed for a major U.S. fashion retailer how different social media mentions, together with firm-initiated marketing actions (TV, radio, circulars, and paid search) drive retail traffic.[11] The social media data is collected by Crimson Hexagon, which indexes over 150 million social media posts per day, including blog posts, forum messages, Facebook posts, and the entire Twitter fire hose of tweets.

Buckets of Love

We chose three conversational themes based on their expected differential effect on traffic and paid media's ability to impact the conversations. The first conversation bucket is about loving the brand (Love WOM). The second bucket contained posts about going to the store or making a purchase (Purchase WOM). The former represents positive brand recommendations, the latter corresponds to an individual's actions influencing others' expected utility. The last conversation bucket held posts about the brand's advertisements or commercials (Ad WOM).

What did we find when we computed the short-term (same-week) and long-term effects of marketing actions and social media topic mentions? In the week of the activity (short-run), all types of WOM conversations increase traffic more than any paid marketing effort, including search engine marketing. Still, the type of WOM is key: Doubling the WOM buzz about the company's ads yields only half the store traffic benefit (13 percent) of doubling of WOM buzz about actual store visits (26 percent). As for online traffic, WOM regarding love for the brand is most effective, with Purchase WOM and Ad WOM tied in second place—all considerably higher than paid marketing actions.

Interestingly, WOM buzz is even more effective for online traffic than increase in organic search. This likely reflects the self-selection of consumers who initiate search. Note, however, that part of this search is also driven by WOM. Likewise, specific marketing actions are driving specific WOM topics, with TV and radio having an immediate impact on Purchase WOM, and circulars having a similar impact on Ad and Love WOM.

Quarterly Dividends

Because of quarterly performance pressures, the retailer was most interested to learn about the effects of WOM and marketing within one quarter. Therefore, we moved beyond the immediate (same-week) effects and calculated the effects within the next thirteen weeks (one quarter). These long-term effects show an even larger benefit of WOM conversations over marketing, reflecting the longer carryover of WOM. First, doubling marketing communication increases store traffic by between 4 and 11 percent. This is consistent with hundreds of studies that reveal average elasticities of 0.05 to 0.10 for advertising. The long-term store traffic benefits of WOM are an order of magnitude higher, from 1.64 for Ad WOM to 3.55 for Love WOM. In contrast, long-term WOM benefits on online traffic are considerably lower. They are identical to the short-term effects, as we find no significant carry-over benefits.

In sum, our calculations show that a 1 percent change to WOM creates a much higher traffic lift than a 1 percent change in marketing activity. In particular, conversations about Love for the brand pay off, with a short-term elasticity three times higher and a long-term elasticity thirty times higher than the most effective paid marketing effort. Interesting information for the retailer monitoring online WOM, but what can its management do to increase the right WOM?

The retailer uses four main marketing actions: TV ads, radio ads, circulars (print), and paid search ads. In addition to the direct effect marketing efforts have on traffic, they can also have an indirect effect through WOM or search. Table 9–2 shows the breakdown of the total store traffic impact of each marketing action into direct and indirect effects.

The Ripple Effect

Television ads do not just increase store traffic directly (68% of the total impact) but also indirectly by stimulating online site traffic (10%) and Purchase WOM (23%). In contrast, the highly popular circulars indirectly stimulate store traffic mostly through Love WOM and Ad WOM. Some consumers also perform organic searches for the products and categories featured in the circulars, which further benefits store traffic. Consumers are typically exposed to TV and circulars in their homes, where they have easy online access. This is not the case for radio ads, to which most consumers listen while driving. As a result, radio ads directly increase traffic to the physical store, which then leads to Purchase WOM that encourages other consumers to visit the store. Finally, paid search ads do not typically drive consumers directly to the physical store, but are effective in stimulating organic search, online traffic, and all topics of WOM conversations.

On average, the indirect store traffic effect of paid marketing is 38% of the total. Thus, managers substantially underestimate marketing effec-

Table 9–2, Breakdown of the Total Effect of Marketing on Store Traffic

	Store Traffic	Online Traffic	Organic Search	Love WOM	Ad WOM	Purchase WOM
TV	68%	10%	0%	0%	0%	23%
Circulars	63%	6%	8%	12%	11%	0%
Radio	78%	0%	0%	0%	0%	22%
Paid search	38%	7%	11%	18%	14%	13%
Average	62%	6%	5%	7%	6%	14%

tiveness if they consider only the direct traffic effects. A key goal and benefit of paid marketing is its power to stimulate conversations around a brand or product, which then causes a ripple effect that ultimately increases business performance.

In conclusion, the U.S. retailer discovered that content-specific WOM performs better than Facebook and Twitter volume and sentiment metrics in explaining store traffic and online traffic. Among the conversation topics, "Love for the Brand" has a larger long-term traffic effect, but neutral conversations regarding Purchase WOM drive traffic in the short run. Firm-initiated marketing drive online WOM and are a key business driver. Especially paid search, circulars, and TV succeed in stimulating WOM conversations, while radio has mostly a direct effect on traffic and then on Purchase WOM. Thus, paid marketing can help build (love for) the brand online by starting and perpetuating the conversation among consumers.

What role can companies play in this social media world? And even more important, what role should *your* company play? Godes and colleagues[12] distinguish four possible roles: observer, moderator (such as by establishing online communities or referral systems), mediator (connecting consumers directly with one another), and participant (openly taking part in online conversations). They note that the last three roles involve perceived bias and ethical issues, which may form a key obstacle for firms contemplating getting out of the merely passive observer role. Indeed, companies have gotten into serious trouble when the online audience perceives a strong commercial push in social media settings.

However, I see a fifth role for companies—one that avoids ethical issues. Managers can use specific paid marketing actions to stimulate specific WOM content conversations. For instance, for the retailer in the case study above, when an immediate sales boost is needed, radio drives both store traffic and Purchase WOM, and the latter, in turn, quickly translates into traffic. In contrast, when longer-term benefits are important, circulars stimulate Love WOM, which has the highest long-term store traffic elasticity. Note the difference between this role of openly using paid marketing to stimulate WOM and the current practice of directly "seeding" WOM, which runs the risk of consumer backlash.

WRAP-UP AND MANAGER'S MEMO

It's challenging but possible to capture the best online metrics for your company. In this chapter, you've learned that you can apply the insights from previous chapters to the world of the connected customer. However, online marketing is less about control and more about influencing prospective customers to act; it's about monitoring and guiding conversation topics in social media. You've learned that content-integrated actions are better than content-separated actions to guide prospects to your website and to convert them into buyers. Beyond measuring volume and sentiment in social media, you saw how tracking the conversation topic yields specific insights, and how different marketing actions (offline and online) can drive different conversations. Fortunately, it's rather easy and inexpensive to experiment with marketing changes online. Try it out for yourself!

In September 2012, the University of Muenster brought together a wonderful team of European and American researchers and managers for the Social Media Thought Leader Summit.[13] As a group, we distilled the following seven rules for including online and social metrics.

MANAGER'S MEMO

SEVEN SECRETS OF ONLINE METRICS

1. **Rule #1: Dynamics are more important than static metrics.** Traditional media are predominantly measured in states, not processes or dynamics. However, as customer-initiated contacts and social media are more akin to living organisms, managers should pay elevated attention to (real-time) dynamics rather than actual states or levels. For example, the number of total "likes" is not really important per se if the activity of these "likes" is very

low. To the contrary, low activity combined with high cumulative "likes" suggests a previously interesting, but currently "dead" site.

2. **Rule #2: Let a thousand flowers bloom: Divergence over convergence.** For traditional media, organizations thrive on convergence toward better states reflected in metrics. For instance, the higher "brand sympathy" across the population, the better. In social media, however, such convergence is dangerous. When your offer gets a unanimous five out of five stars, delighted customers stop to post reviews that do not appear to add value. Only reviewers who are less happy, or want to stand out, will post, dragging your ratings down. Niche brands in particular may thrive on adversity in social media as differentiation increases and reinforces the identification of its core users.

3. **Rule #3: Put quantity and quality metrics on your dashboard.** Many organizations are proud of their high fan numbers or followers and measure success through the growth of this figure or its actual number. However, apart from trying to signal popularity, that figure may not be of much use. Social media thrive on activity, not "dead" volume. Hence, in this case it's the engaged fans or followers you want to take care of. And this number will not grow by a series of sweepstakes or questions like "how is the weather in XYZ," but organically over time through honest, frequent, and relevant interaction.

4. **Rule #4: Heisenberg rocks: Observing a social media metric will change it!** Just as in physics, we observe that once someone establishes a metric to measure something in social media, users will start to game it. Think of Klout scores, Google or YouTube rankings, etc. Once people realize that these are important metrics that are aligned with profits, or with social, intellectual, or cultural value, they start to game them. When constructing a social media dashboard or metric, you always need to make sure to design a counterbalancing force. Some precautionary aspects built into such metrics may entail such feats as actual activity ratios rather than just counting numbers of (eventually "artificial" or "dead") backlinks.

5. **Rule #5: Ying and Yang: Understand the principles of balance in social systems.** Social media platforms are still evolving in

terms of user base and usage levels. This may distort assessments as user growth will eventually slow as diffusion approaches saturation levels, especially in terms of relative increases. Also, heavy users of social media tend to adopt earlier than people with lower usage. Accordingly, average usage time may eventually go down over time as more people join in. These dynamics should hold at all levels of analysis, from the total network down to brand hubs within those media. For instance, if you assign a subsection of the dashboard to the brand's activists, then these metrics should be relatively comparable over time even as the number of low-involvement users keeps growing.

6. **Rule #6: Don't confuse urgency with importance.** Social media are living organisms. Accordingly, dashboards will always keep on blinking in real time. Deviations, even substantial ones, are the rule rather than the exception. Traditional firms are often overwhelmed by the pulse of social media and interfere too soon and inappropriately, pushing the situation into a tailspin. Dashboard developers and users need to extract and interpret the essence of conversations and sentiments among the public, but also identify a corridor of comfort that is defined via heterogeneity and dynamics around crucial metrics. Within this comfort zone, organizations need to let go.

7. **Rule #7: Strive for influence, not control.** As you cannot control other people, you cannot control social media. As in real life, you need friends and attorneys that speak on your behalf. These need not be many, but they must be trustworthy and influential ones. Together with Rule # 3, this means it is the quality and level of engagement of your fan base that counts, not just its size. Even for what we call "seemingly" low-involvement products, such as toothpaste or tissues, there are a sufficient number of activists that an organization can engage with. A case in point is the "roll under/roll over" campaign by Cottonelle toilet tissue: The company allowed people across the United States to discuss and vote on this "important" issue. Any social media dashboard should reflect this insight.

CHAPTER 10

Emerging Markets Frontier: Metrics Across Countries

Marketing principles are universally applicable, and the marketer's task is the same, whether applied in Dimebox, Texas or Katmandu, Nepal.

—CATEORA AND HESS, 1966

Consumers in emerging markets are more likely to talk about any kind of online advert than their counterparts in mature markets.

—MINDSHARE, 2011

WHICH QUOTE DO YOU BELIEVE? Marketing has seen a long debate about whether marketing programs should be globally integrated or locally customized. On the global integration side of the boxing ring, Theodore Levitt[1] assumes that differences across cultures and languages are small enough as to justify a standard marketing mix across countries. On the side of local customization, many qualitative researchers argue that each country/region (sometimes even each town within a country) is different and deserves a different marketing approach. My view is in between: I've learned that countries differ in systematic ways, which can be captured by institutional, cultural, and economic (ICE) dimensions. Once you break the ICE, consumers will appreciate your adapted approach to solve their problems, while your company will keep its efficiency by "worldwide learning,"[2] that is, applying the learning from one country to similar countries.

Why is this important for our marketing analytics dashboard?

Remember from Chapter 8 how marketing responsiveness and sales conversion metrics are important criteria for dashboard priorities? Differences in metrics' responsiveness to marketing actions, and in conversion into sales, suggest different branding strategies in emerging versus mature markets. You may be strong in mature markets, but struggle in emerging markets. For instance, Procter & Gamble knows it has to catch up with its rival Unilever in emerging markets—it's the only way to keep global growth promises for the company. Likewise for durables, General Motors and Peugeot struggled to obtain a share of the Chinese market due to *cultural misunderstandings*.[3] On the other hand, brands from emerging markets, such as Lenovo and Haier, struggle to succeed in mature markets because they lack a strong *emotional connection* with their customers.[4] As an international company manager, therefore, what you basically need is to figure out how customers in specific markets feel, think, and behave in response to your marketing actions.

THE NEED FOR STANDARDIZED, GLOBAL METRICS

It's important to enforce identical metrics globally, and equally important to allow local strategies to improve them. For instance, the global business communications company in the case study in Chapter 7 ("The Right Call #1: What Is a Qualified Lead?") insists that all countries have the same definition of performance drivers, in particular, the so-called "qualified leads" that marketing passes on to sales. However, this does not mean that the same marketing action has the same power to increase qualified leads in each country, nor does it mean that qualified leads convert at the same rate into sales contracts in every country. The first is called the "marketing responsiveness"; the second, the "sales conversion" of an LKPI.

In this chapter, I focus on end consumers (rather than retailers and trade partners—which also differ by market) and share with you my experience on which metrics matter most in emerging and in mature markets. The key insight is that consumers in such markets tend to both think/feel differently about your marketing actions and to react differently to their thoughts and attitudes.

Your own analysis of these differences in your industry will be most valuable to your company. My specific findings in the personal care industry may offer some inspiration. Figure 10–1 shows our specific findings, which I explain in the next sections. First, communication awareness (that important overlooked key leading performance indicator discussed in Chapter 8) is more responsive to advertising in emerging markets than in mature markets. In contrast, brand attitudes consideration and liking are less responsive to marketing actions in emerging markets. Finally, sales conversion of brand liking is lower in emerging markets than in mature ones.

This chapter explores and explains these findings in two ways. First, I outline the factors that drive differences in consumer reactions. In particular, emerging market consumers are expected to differ from their counterparts in mature markets due to the lack of regulative protection, collectivist culture, and low income. Second, I discuss the practical consequences of different consumer reactions in terms of communication awareness, brand consideration, and brand liking. Finally, a case study details how one brand derived specific insights for the effectiveness of its advertising actions. Taken together, this chapter explains why you should expect different reactions from emerging and

Figure 10–1, Emerging and Mature Markets: Responsiveness and Sales Conversion

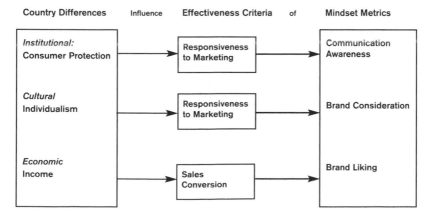

mature market consumers. Most important, it enables you to decide which metrics to put on your dashboard to successfully run your company in an emerging market.

To illustrate these differences in emerging and mature markets, we focus on three main mindset metrics:

1. **Communication awareness:** To what extent consumers are aware of your marketing communication.

2. **Brand consideration:** To what extent consumers include your brand in their consideration sets.

3. **Brand liking:** To what extent consumers like your brand.

For marketing actions to effectively change behavior, three things must take place:

1. Consumers must become aware of marketing communication. This refers to an increase in *communication awareness* in response to your marketing communication.

2. They must be open to change their minds and hearts. This refers to the responsiveness of brand attitudes, such as *brand consideration* and *brand liking*. We can think of consideration set inclusion as capturing consumers' minds, and of liking as capturing consumers' hearts.

3. They must be willing to consequently change their buying patterns. This refers to the conversion of a change in heart or mind to a change in *behavior*—that is, buying your brand.

In the first two steps, you may observe how effective your *marketing actions influence* your consumers' awareness levels, minds, and hearts. The final step captures the sales effect of any change in the consumers' mindset metrics. This is known as "two-step flow"; it has been the dominant theory on how communication influences behavior since the 1950s.[5]

How and why do emerging markets differ from mature markets in the marketing responsiveness and sales conversion of their mindset metrics? As shown earlier in Figure 10–1, the answer lies in the institutional, cultural, and economic differences across countries. For many marketers, especially important are consumer protection as the institutional factor, individualism/collectivism as the cultural factor, and income level as the economic factor. These factors strongly affect the marketing responsiveness and sales conversion of communication awareness, brand consideration, and brand liking.

CONSUMER PROTECTION LOWERS MARKETING RESPONSIVENESS OF CONSUMER AWARENESS

Across the globe, consumers do not like risk and tend to search for more information if perceived risk is high. However, the extent of risk is very different in many emerging and mature markets. Emerging markets lack the consumer protection typically found in mature markets, including recourse against defective products; and buyers have little access to independent consumer organizations and publications that provide unbiased information. In contrast, consumers in mature markets are relatively carefree buying supermarket items, as they enjoy strong protection and often assume that all brands offered by mainstream retailers deliver at least basic quality. Moreover, goods can often be returned "no questions asked" in mature markets, which further lowers consumer purchase worries.

How do differences in consumer protection affect the consumers' purchase process? Study after study shows that consumers in emerging markets pay more attention to marketing communication. For instance, 74 percent of consumers in Latin America (77 percent in Brazil) trust television advertising compared to only 49 percent in the EU.[6] Similarly, 82 percent of consumers in Latin America agree with the statement that "by providing information, advertising allows for better consumer choices" compared to 50 percent in the EU. In other words, the information function of marketing is higher in emerging markets.[7] In the caveat emptor (buyer beware) environment of the emerging markets, the buyer is the main responsible party for ensuring that product quality meets minimum standards. The desire to avoid poor-quality products induces consumers to attend more to communication regarding the quality of brands. This was confirmed in a recent study by my colleagues Erguncu and Yildirim and myself.[8] The three findings, discussed in the next few pages, come from that study.

Finding #1: Communication awareness is more responsive to marketing communication for emerging market consumers than for mature market consumers.

In other words, your marketing dollars are more likely to get noticed in emerging markets than in mature markets. But how effective are they in moving hearts and minds?

INDIVIDUALISM INCREASES MARKETING RESPONSIVENESS OF BRAND CONSIDERATION AND LIKING

The relation between the individual and the group is directly reflected onto consumers' brand choice decisions. People in *individualist* cultures (e.g., in the United States and most European countries) believe that the individual is the most important unit. They are self-oriented, make their decisions based on individual needs, and independently pursue their own ideas and preferences. In contrast, people in *collectivistic* cultures (e.g., China, India, and Latin America) believe that the group is the most important unit. They are group-oriented—their decisions are based on what is best for the group—and because they identify with the group and participate in its shared way of life, they find meaning in life largely through social relationships. For instance, L'Oreal's branding strategy and forty-year-old slogan "because I am worth it" has been successful in mature markets, but not in emerging markets. The main reason is a failure to recognize emerging market consumers' tendency to value the opinions of their friends, families, and peers when they make their brand choice decisions.[9] The company's 2011 change to "because we are worth it" better reflects emerging market realities.

How does culture affect the marketing responsiveness of consumers' hearts and minds? Living in an individualist culture, most mature market consumers see themselves as independent and distinct from the group and, accordingly, they place a high value on uniqueness, individual accomplishments, and personal achievement. As a result, they should feel free to change their own brand attitudes substantially based on marketing communications. In contrast, most emerging market consumers see themselves as part of a larger group, and accordingly, they value connectedness and conformity and are integrated into strong, cohesive in-groups. Thus, they should be less willing to change their attitudes based solely on marketing communications. Instead, their attitude changes are mostly derived from group interactions. In our studies, we find that:

Finding #2: Brand attitudes consideration and liking are less responsive to marketing communications for emerging market consumers than for mature market consumers.

Figure 10–2 shows typical advertising responsiveness figures for the same brands in an emerging versus a mature market.

INCOME INCREASES THE SALES CONVERSION OF BRAND LIKING

Finally, income plays two key roles in how consumers evaluate your brand. First, low-income consumers differ from high-income con-

Figure 10–2, Advertising Responsiveness in an Emerging and a Mature Market

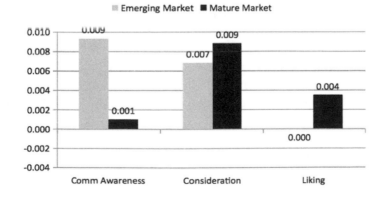

sumers in perceiving a product as a necessity rather than a *luxury*. High-income consumers enjoy the luxury of buying the brands they love. They also differ in the *focus* of their purchase decision, that is, low-income consumers make more rational than emotional purchases. Comparing Malaysia with France, Hult and his colleagues find that consumers in the lower-income country place more importance on tangible attributes, such as price and safety.[10] Thus, while low-income consumers focus on the value and product functionality of your brand, high-income consumers mostly prioritize their emotional connection with your brand.

Emotional brand connection or "'brand love'" is driven by passion, separation distress, romance, mystery, and sensuality. These are recent buzz words in mature markets, where many consumers have the luxury to buy "mysterious" products—at least in relatively inexpensive categories. In contrast, most emerging market consumers base their purchase decisions on functional and trust attributes. Indeed, our studies show that:

Finding #3: Brand liking has a lower sales conversion for emerging market than for mature market consumers.

Figure 10–3 shows typical sales conversion numbers in an emerging and a mature market.

The findings discussed above are played out in the case study that follows.[11]

Figure 10–3, Sales Conversion of Mindset Metrics in an Emerging and a Mature Market

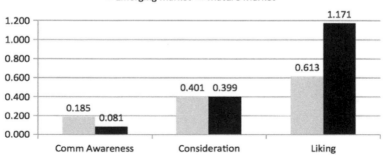

HOW ADVERTISING EFFECTS DIFFER IN AN EMERGING AND A MATURE MARKET

A personal care brand is particularly concerned about its sales performance in two countries: its main mature market, the United Kingdom, and its most important emerging market, Brazil. The brand's relative price point, positioning, and market share are similar in both countries, but it faces more and stronger competition in the mature market. Its advertising message was developed globally and tested as relevant to consumers in both countries. However, brand managers were unsure how much of the global advertising budget to spend in the mature versus the emerging market. In the mature market, both consumers and retailers reacted very positively to the ad campaign, while the emerging market remained largely silent. Therefore, management intuition was to give more money to the mature market.

An analysis applied vector autoregressive (VAR) models to monthly data series in each market. Managers were surprised by the advertising-sales effects shown in Figure 10–4. It shows the sales elasticity (percentage of sales increase for a 1 percent ad budget increase) for the mature market (light gray line) and the emerging market (dark gray line). The graphs display the effects that are statistically significant from zero (the baseline before the advertising increase).

In the mature market, advertising gave a strong immediate boost to sales within the same month, but sales go back to baseline afterwards. In contrast, advertising took a few months to translate into sales in the emerging market—but once it did, sales stayed at the new higher level even while the ad campaign was over. How to explain these differences? We next looked at the marketing responsiveness and sales conversion of the dashboard metrics of brand consideration and liking. In the mature market, the successful ad campaign worked only through brand liking, which went up the same month but then went back to baseline the next month. Mature market consumers are fickle, and successful competitors reacted with their own brand love campaigns. In contrast, the ad campaign did not immediately boost any metric in the emerging market. Instead, it stimulated prospective consumers to ask around about the brand, as reflected in the offline and online word-of-mouth metrics you

Figure 10–4, Advertising–Sales Elasticity Over Time for an Emerging and a Mature Market

read about in Chapter 9. Once other consumers responded positively to questions about the brand, brand consideration rose in the market and stayed at its higher level. The sales conversion of brand consideration is substantial in the emerging market, so the higher consideration turned into a gift that kept on giving.

Management learned that the same sales-boosting ad campaign had very different effects in its native mature market and its main emerging market. In the mature market, the sales boost was immediate but temporary, because it went through the fickle metric of brand liking. In the emerging market, the sales boost took longer to materialize because it required a word-of-mouth process among prospective consumers. However, the sales boost also was longer-lasting, driven by a long-term boost to brand consideration. The CMO shifted ad dollars to exploit this opportunity window for the emerging market, and searched for different options to boost long-term sales in the mature market. Moreover, the company decided to reward the emerging market managers based on increases in consideration, a key leading performance indicator in that market.

WRAP-UP AND MANAGER'S MEMO

To beat the challenge of selling to emerging market consumers and to accelerate the penetration of these markets, brands from mature markets must achieve global scale and local focus. In particular, you must offer emerging consumers different value propositions by modifying your business and marketing strategies—and when possible, you must seek to decrease your costs. With better understanding of the needs—institutional, cultural, and economic (ICE)—of emerging consumers and adapting your business models to serve them more efficiently and effectively, your growth can be sustainable.

On the flip side, brands born in emerging markets should be wary of carrying their assumptions into mature markets. For example, Hyundai now recognizes the need in the U.S. market to move beyond a "left-brain choice" (value, fuel economy, lengthy warranty) and started to show ads that "aim to add an emotional connection and remind people that buying a Hyundai isn't just a rational choice".[12]

In a nutshell, measure your metrics in exactly the same way in every country, but allow for different priorities depending on which metric responds more to marketing, and converts more to sales in a specific situation.

MANAGER'S MEMO

BREAKING THE ICE IN INTERNATIONAL MARKETS

1. Emerging market consumers are more attentive to marketing communications than their mature market counterparts, who tend to block out marketing communication. Emerging market consumers often actively and carefully search for information on brands.

   COROLLARY: Prioritize reach over frequency in your marketing budget. Aim to ensure that relevant consumer groups are aware of and consider the brand for purchase, instead of repeating the same message over and over in the hope of breaking through to a few consumers.

2. Consumers living in a collectivist culture are less responsive to advertising in their consideration and liking of the advertised

brand. They highly value the opinions, experiences, and advice of others to consider or like a brand.

COROLLARY: Patience is gold in emerging markets; managers should immediately track whether consumers received the message, but then they need to give the social influence process time to flourish. A pulse of ad spending should allow marketing communication to start the social influence process, which then requires little if any further stimulation due to the effect of word-of-mouth and the staying power of brand consideration.

3. Lower income among consumers reduces the sales conversion of brand liking. A brand does not need be "loved" in an emerging market, but it does need to be known and respected. A great example is Lenovo in China.

   COROLLARY: Aim to be Mr. Right instead of Mr. Right Now. Your marketing communication should highlight where and why your brand dominates and can be trusted. Mystery, sensuality, and intimacy are just icing on the cake—and often unnecessary.

Once you break the ICE with emerging market consumers, the future looks bright indeed.

CHAPTER 11

Design the Layout and Dashboard Prototype

I saw the angel in the marble and carved until I set him free.

—MICHELANGELO, SIXTEENTH CENTURY

ONCE YOU KNOW WHICH METRICS should be on your analytic dashboard and how they are related, it is time to put it all together and decide on the design that will best communicate insights to users. The bad news: even the best analytics can go to waste if you make ugly mistakes in dashboard design. The good news: there are hundreds of articles, videos, and websites with good and bad design examples and guidelines to help you. In this chapter, we organize these rich guidelines to nudge you in the right direction regarding *dashboard structure*, *data display*, and *visualization*.

DASHBOARD STRUCTURE: SEVEN MUST-HAVES

The ultimate aim of a marketing analytic dashboard is to help make better decisions. Dashboards need to be designed/customized for their users, to support their decisions, responsibilities, and level in the organization. Still, experience has shown several general criteria across industries and organization levels. An effective dashboard structure is typically simple, clear, compact, readable, insightful, interactive—and it leads to action. If in addition to these seven must-have characteristics, it can also be flexible, mobile, and able to connect to real-time data, so much the better.

The last three factors have specific benefits but also substantial costs. Flexible dashboards allow users to change the structure according to their needs. Mobile dashboards are accessible from any platform. Finally, the ability to connect to real-time data is key when users need the very latest information (such as the most popular executions of display ads during an expensive field experiment). You can decide whether the costs are worth the benefits based on your work in the previous dashboard steps.

The seven must-haves, in contrast, are virtually free (in hard currency) but do require some careful attention to detail. The best way to illustrate them is to go through some better and worse examples.

The Right Way

Let's start with the Inofec Right Chair dashboard we met in Chapter 1. This company wanted to maximize profits over time by allocating money over four marketing channels at the daily level. As the dashboard was designed for a hands-on CEO, it focuses on how and when allocating marketing dollars across the major instruments leads to higher profits. Figure 11–1 displays a screenshot of the dashboard.

Figure 11–1, A Good Dashboard Structure: Inofec

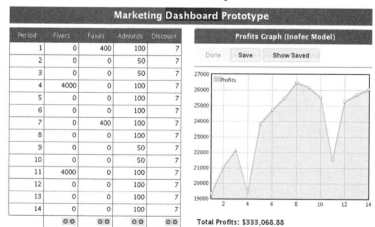

Note how neatly this dashboard meets the essential criteria:

1. **Simple:** only shows total money to each of the four marketing channels, not the details within each channel.

2. **Clear:** only two soft colors are used: blue for action, beige for results. (You will find this and all the other figures in this chapter on my website—notthesizeofthedata.com—in color. To get the most out of this chapter, I suggest you access it on a portable device while you are reading.)

3. **Compact:** only the first fourteen days of planning, which is the typical cycle.

4. **Readable:** all labels are clearly readable, even from this small screenshot.

5. **Insightful:** the size and timing of profits are key insights the user needs.

6. **Interactive:** the user can multiply budgets with a single button, or type in any number.

7. **Leading to action:** through visual comparison of the profit impact of different scenarios.

Our seven criteria are closely related. Dashboard content should be organized in an efficient and meaningful way. A dashboard should not be cluttered with too much data (efficiency), and the sequence, layout, and presentation of data should facilitate comprehension, lead to analysis, and ultimately to action (effectiveness). Figure 11–2 shows an example of how *not* to do it—courtesy of Zach Gemignani

This dashboard is overwhelming (not simple) and unreadable, which destroys the insights and the call to action that a user may have gained with a better structure.

Figure 11–2, An Inefficient and Ineffective Dashboard Structure

Source: Gemignani, Zach (2009). A Guide to Creating Dashboards People Will Love to Use. Part 3: Information Design. Dashboard Insight, November 11, 2009.

The Right Stuff

Beyond the right structure in each screenshot, dashboards should also display the right criteria in their structure of multiple screenshots. For example, the dashboard shown in Figure 11–3 compactly displays (a) the funnel of website visits leading to sales conversions, (b) revenue versus marketing cost in each month, and (c) four key performance indicators and their acceptable range (in green). In a drop-down menu, the user can select different products and different time periods. By clicking on different folders, the user can zoom in on marketing costs, web banners, and website performance.

Structure Informs Decisions

The structure of a dashboard shapes the way its users look at a business problem and see the big picture. It can predefine a dashboard user's understanding of a situation and it frames decisions based on this understanding.

When working on a dashboard structure, you should aim to both promote the positive and to reduce the negative.

Positive—Is the structure logical and does it foster quick understanding of dashboard content?

Negative—Does the dashboard layout confuse users and lead to wrong conclusions?

Ac-Cen-Tchu-Ate the Positive

What are some options for a *logical structure*? Time and place are straightforward; many dashboards are organized by the sequence of events or actions over time (as in Figure 11–3) or across regions, products, or functions within the company (reflecting the organizational structure the user is familiar with). If you have brought in the analytics, you can also group your data according to *cause-and-effect* relations—which is both insightful and leads to action. The Inofec dashboard in Figure 11–1 is a good example. If you have different users at different levels in the organization, think about the hierarchy of decisions as a guideline for the hierarchy of the dashboard. Senior managers may

Figure 11–3, An Effective Dashboard Structure

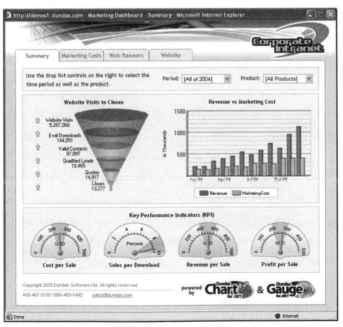

Source: Dundas, "Interactive Dashboard Samples," www.dundas.com/gallery/sample-dashboards/.

need to allocate budgets over regions or products, brand managers over marketing channels, and operational managers over different groups of paid search terms. These different levels of needed information and action insights can be rolled up into a recognizable hierarchy of dashboard views, with logical and consistent links between them.

E-Lim-I-Nate the Negative

As for avoiding the negative, we recommend you to lower the barrier to entry for new users, especially at the initial stages of dashboard implementation, and not overload a dashboard with functions and properties, especially those that require training and are time-consuming.

The popular saying "Keep it simple, stupid!" (KISS) certainly applies to dashboard design. Whenever you add another function, you will need to provide a clear and concise description for it. For example, the decision to include or omit an annotation function on a dashboard depends on the dashboard target audience's requirements and usage patterns. Think about your dashboard as Michelangelo thought about his David masterpiece: Cut away all the superfluous marble bits to set the angel free.

DATA DISPLAY ON THE DASHBOARD

Once you have your structure in place, you have to make key decisions on how to display the data. First of all, you will need to think of where to position the most important information on a dashboard. Multiple studies show that people tend to scan a page from the top left to the top right and down the left side. This means that the *upper part of your dashboard is the right place to put the most critical information*. In fact, such positioning is typical for dashboard design best practices.

In addition, *white space* in dashboard interface design is important and too often neglected. If you maximize dashboard real estate, you should also increase white space—without it the nonwhite dashboard content has less impact. Stuffing the dashboard with too much information reduces clarity, and diverts attention from the most critical data.

It may be painful not to include another chart into a dashboard, but it really helps the user.

An example of displaying too much on the dashboard is shown in Figure 11–4.

Figure 11–4, "Data Puke" Dashboard

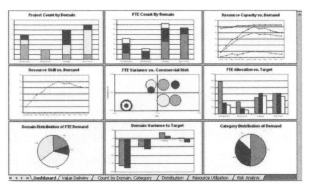

Source: Elliot, Jenny (2011): "Effective Dashboards: The Biggest & Prettiest doesn't always win," blog.crossview.com/effective-dashboards-the-biggest-prettiest-doesnt-always-win/.

Nine different graphs! The dashboard designer wanted to cram too much information on this page. This is overwhelming and counterproductive. Instead, reduce the number of graphs and provide some textual information, as is done in the marketing costs view of the dashboard in Figure 11–5.

Jennifer Veesenmeyer, COO of Stratigent, has excellent advice on dashboard data display.[1] Here's my version of her "seven deadly dashboard sins."

1. Lack of focus on the goal (facilitate analysis rather than monitoring performance).
2. Display all data without insight.
3. Limit data sources to your website only (if your business is multichannel, your dashboard should be too).
4. Too intensive to update.
5. Lack of data context (provide meaningful benchmarks, use size for importance).

Figure 11–5, An Effective Display of Marketing Cost Data

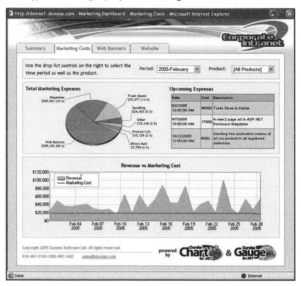

Source: Dundas, "Interactive Dashboard Samples" www.dundas.com/gallery/sample-dashboards/.

6. Use poor visuals that are hard to read or understand (don't develop your dashboard before you've designed it).

7. Separate the metrics from the business objectives the user should care about.

DATA VISUALIZATION

Visualization is an important benefit of many dashboard displays, and should be considered carefully. Make sure the visuals you select are not just eye-pleasing, but also efficiently relay the correct message. There are numerous visualization tools that can be customized to suit your communication goal. Your task is to choose a graph that will be the most effective way to present your data and that will not mislead its users. As always, it's key to understand where the user is coming from. Our ten rules on dashboard visualization start from the user perspective[2]:

1. **Highlight key metrics and areas that require attention**. Use

thresholds to trigger alerts and bring user attention to (potential) trouble areas. Such alerts should translate key data on a dashboard and lead to proactive management—and to action! Figure 11–6 presents an example of a threshold-triggered alert in use on a dashboard. (And although you cannot tell from this black and white illustration, the alert is in bright reds and yellow; your house is clearly on fire!)

2. **Deemphasize areas and objects**. Use plain and unobtrusive colors to define dashboard borders and backgrounds in order to let users focus on key information displayed.

3. **Categorize information with color**. Identify the types of information your dashboard contains, and mark each type with an appropriate color. The latter can help users recognize the type of information they are looking at right away and read it accordingly. A good example is dark green: it usually denotes monetary values and therefore it is easily and instantly decoded as such by any business professional.

4. **Identify dashboard type and level**. Different dashboard background and title colors can also help users determine what types of information they are looking at. For example, once again, dark green is an appropriate color to frame or mark financial information on marketing dashboards. Further, the level of a dashboard, C-level or senior level, for example, can

Figure 11–6, A Simple Alert Triggered by a Threshold

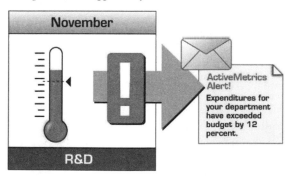

Source: PureShare Whitepaper. Metrics Dashboard Design: Designing Effective Metrics Management Dashboards. www.pureshare.com/resources/resource_files/pureshare_dashboard_design.pdf.

be indicated in a dashboard title. By doing so you will make sure that your dashboard reaches its specific audience.

5. **Indicate the time when data was retrieved and the dashboard was updated**. In most cases, time is the key to reading the data displayed on a dashboard; its presence may guide dashboard users toward the right conclusion, just as its absence may confuse and mislead them. Therefore, ensure that this information is present—but don't crowd the dashboard display.

6. **Apply commonly used colors, symbols, and navigation tools**. For example, red is the color usually used to mark something that requires attention, highlight key data, and create an alert. Use red when, for instance, sales fall below a preset threshold. Likewise, use widely accepted symbols, such as caution signs, rather than developing new symbols that users will have to learn. Don't reinvent the wheel—or anything else. The organization of your dashboard should be clear, consistent, and coherent.

7. **Homogenize dashboard templates**. Build and apply a limited set of templates that will be consistent in color, symbols, and navigation, and use them throughout an organization. It will significantly ease dashboard user comprehension and will accelerate user adoption rate.

8. **Present data on dashboards in a consistent way**. Place each type of data (a trend, a percentage, or an absolute number) in the same place across all your corporate dashboards, and be consistent in choosing the same type of display for the same data on each dashboard.

9. **Use meaningful and descriptive titles**. Give preference to descriptive over cryptic or symbolic titles, as the former are generally more intuitive and clear. And I'm a great believer in assigning labels to various dashboard sets. But one caveat— don't overuse titles and labels, as they can divert the dashboard user from the essential information being displayed.

10. **Avoid cluttering dashboards** and dashboard displays with
    unnecessary properties, such as 3-D effects that crowd the
    dashboard interface rather than add value to the information
    it contains (see Figure 11–7).

Figure 11–7, Unnecessary Visual Effects Hinder Readability

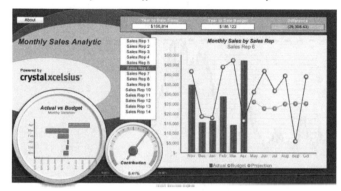

Source: Few, Stephen (2007). Dashboard Confusion Revisited. Perceptual Edge, Visual Business
Intelligence Newsletter, March 2007.

Yes, that's a big bunch of rules I've thrown at you. But the more
closely you heed them, the better your dashboard will be! Now let's take
a look at how Procter & Gamble did it, courtesy of Thomas Davenport,[3]
in the case study that follows.

CASE STUDY

DATA VISUALIZATION AT PROCTER & GAMBLE

Procter & Gamble (P&G) is known worldwide for its consistent and efficient marketing of fast-moving consumer goods. Household names
include Ariel laundry detergent, Bounty paper towels, Braun electronics,
Charmin bathroom tissue, Crest toothpaste, Duracell batteries, Febreze
freshener, Gillette razors, Head & Shoulders shampoo, Iams pet foods,
Olay beauty products, Pampers diapers, Tide laundry detergent, Vicks
cold medicine, and Wella hair care.

   The company is also known for its consistent data visualization. One
example is the heat map in Figure 11–8, showing how P&G's products

Figure 11–8, P&G's Heat Map

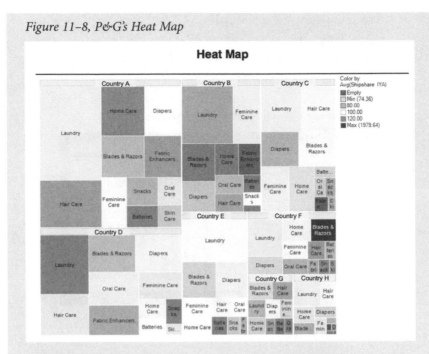

rank in market share for each of their respective country markets. Because we are limited to black and white here, I urge you to explore the color version, which can be found on my website: notthesizeofthedata.com. In this heat map, the size of the box indicates the importance of growing that market share to overall company performance. This fits with my Foreword to Laura Patterson's *Marketing Metrics in Action* (Racom Communications, 2008):

> I believe dashboards should not just flag poor performance, but also exceptional performance and its causes. Such opportunities may then be fully exploited by scaling up investment in related activities and aligning the organization to fulfill the resulting demand growth. Far from extinguishing innovation and creativity, such dashboards thus help marketing take smarter risks by assessing experimental projects and forecasting the profit potential of bigger, bolder initiatives.

> Indeed, P&G marketers are encouraged to compare performance not just with targets or competitors, but with the potential of what could have been achieved.

The heat map data display is more action-oriented and helpful to decision makers than previous tools. As Guy Peri (IT Director) explains: "Historically, we used to celebrate businesses or initiatives being "green" or spend time on businesses/initiatives that were red—when in comparison to the broader portfolio, those businesses/initiatives were relatively immaterial to the overall performance. With visual analytics, we are able to quickly focus business decision makers on the business issues that are material."[4]

Note how the heat map illustrates many of our ten rules on dashboard visualization. (If you haven't already gone to a website to see Figure 11–8 in color, do so now—really.) It highlights key metrics and areas that need attention: in this case, using both size and color (rule 1). It de-emphasizes areas and objects: these are not visible in the P&G heat map (rule 2). It categorizes with appropriate colors (green, red, and gray) (rules 3 through 6). It has homogenized templates and presents data in a consistent way: the data visualization is exactly the same across the world, making it easy to share ideas and get expats started in a new country (rules 7 and 8). And finally, it uses meaningful titles and avoids cluttering: even though it shows a lot of information, the data visualization is meaningful and focuses attention on areas for improvement (rules 9 and 10).

In one sentence, P&G's CIO Filippo Passerini calls it "getting beyond the what to the why and the how."[5] Indeed, the real goal of visual displays is to direct management attention to where it is most needed. Data visualization helps decision makers get past the data itself to start thinking and discussing about why something happened and how they can act to improve the situation.

WRAP-UP AND MANAGER'S MEMO

The major task of dashboard design is to direct attention to the right insights and to help decision makers "get past the what" to the why and how to take action. We firmly believe a minimalist approach is best for dashboard design. Start with a customized and simple structure, respect the time of typical dashboard users who are busy professionals who may not have time to learn the complex functions of a dashboard and yet they want to see a meaningful synthesis of the big picture, their individual performance and how they can improve both. The P&G case study is a wonderful illustration of how data visualization helps.

Here are our ten rules of dashboard visualization.

MANAGER'S MEMO

TEN RULES OF DASHBOARD VISUALIZATION

1. Highlight key metrics and areas that require attention.

2. Deemphasize areas and objects.

3. Categorize information with color.

4. Identify dashboard type and level.

5. Indicate time when data was retrieved and updated.

6. Apply commonly used colors, symbols, and navigation tools.

7. Homogenize dashboard templates.

8. Present data on dashboards in a consistent way.

9. Use meaningful and descriptive titles.

10. Avoid cluttering dashboards and dashboard displays with unnecessary properties.

PART FOUR

Live Your Marketing Analytics Dashboard

CHAPTER 12

Launch and Renewal of the Marketing Analytics Dashboard

I'm lucky. I have a dashboard where I can track and optimize the entire marketing process from brand positioning all the way to customer demand—in real time. It's great input for decision making. That said, we can't let metrics completely displace our judgment and experience.

—JONATHAN BECHER, CMO OF SAP

DASHBOARD IMPLEMENTATION ROADMAP

You have come a long way: initiating, planning, and designing a marketing analytic dashboard. Once it comes to implementation though... it does not get easier. Like any important change in your organization, dashboard implementation involves many people and processes, with many potential roadblocks along the way.

In our experience, the dashboard launch is the most challenging part after metrics selection. You need to plan the project launch very carefully and know specifically what aspects of the dashboard implementation should be taken care of before putting the dashboard into action for the first time.

At this point the project stakeholders should be very clear about the project expectations and deliverables during the first three to six months of the dashboard launch. To the list of steps you must go through on your dashboard journey we have added three more to the first seven, which were discussed in earlier chapters.

1. **Communicate the dashboard initiative and get managerial support.** This is one of the most critical steps for your project, since at this point your company's management decides whether to give you the green light or not. Check out our advice in Chapter 3 and be sure you effectively communicate your dashboard initiative from the very start. Your major goal here is to obtain managerial support for the project, and your success depends heavily on the way you present your dashboard idea and its usefulness to the company.

2. **Identify the project team.** You should clearly determine who will be actively involved in the dashboard initiative implementation (discussed in Chapter 4). This includes identifying who will be the project stakeholders overall, who will be the executive sponsor of the project, who will be the primary users of the dashboard, etc. You will need to be able to determine the right people to start and manage the project, and you also must handle the challenge of motivating them. Employee engagement and managerial support are key factors at this stage.

   Especially for analytics dashboards, you will need to get the IT department on your side (Chapter 5). You will work on technology decisions for your dashboard application in close collaboration with IT employees. We recommend that you start considering various technology options as soon as top management approves your project. Your company needs and budget will be key factors in the technology decision.

3. **Define the dashboard project scope.** Chapters 3, 4, and 5 help you define the scope of the dashboard project. Given the vision, the team's opinions, and the IT support, what is the scope of the dashboard project? Specifically, what it is to deliver, and what it is not? What lies within its objectives?

What financial, human, and time resources will be allocated? As a matter of fact, budget plays a defining role in determining the project scope, which in turn guides the later steps of establishing the data measurement system and obtaining the desired metrics. Therefore you will need to set realistic objectives for your dashboard application—you will need to find the right balance between meeting the dashboard users' needs and staying within the agreed-upon budget limits. At the same time, the dashboard project scope should help the business strategy of your company. It should fit the company's strategic objectives and goals. This is just the right time to remind you of the involved discussion on project goal alignment in Chapter 3.

4. **Establish the data measurement system.** You should be able to answer the following questions (remember Chapter 6?) at this stage:

   - Where is the data?
   - Who is responsible for data collection?
   - Who is managing the database?
   - How mature is the database?
   - How complex are the data, database, data collection, and database management?
   - Is the data homogenized? How much do datasets vary?

Very often, you will find yourself collaborating with employees from different departments and organizational levels in order to get complete information on the database in place. Also, after you have decided on key metrics to be included in the dashboard, you should be ready that it may take days to gather the relevant data for a single key performance indicator.

On the other hand, it may be often the case that the data is not there and there is no database in place. Chapter 6 helps you to establish a measurement system and build a database relevant to your industry and your business, in particular.

5. **Gather requirements and candidate metrics.** Once the scope of the dashboard project has been defined, the process of requirements gathering begins. You will need to interview the key stakeholders and primary dashboard users to identify their needs and expectations. Asking them to identify metrics that will serve them better is killing two birds with one stone. Chapter 7 offers you details on how to approach these interviews. You should accumulate this knowledge and transform it in an information platform that will serve as the dashboard project requirements' and candidate metrics' storage. Keep in mind that you will refer to this storage quite frequently; therefore its content should be easily accessible and comprehensible.

6. **Select and define key leading performance indicators (KLPIs).** Chapter 8 helps you with the hardest task for many organizations: identifying the most important metrics and relating them to performance outcomes. This is especially challenging if the dashboard needs to cover both traditional and emerging channels such as online social media (Chapter 9), and even more so if it covers both mature and emerging markets (Chapter 10) as well.

7. **Design and construct a prototype.** Chapter 11 discussed specific design elements of the dashboard, based on requirements and selected metrics. This stage will be heavily operational, and therefore excellent execution and management are the key success factors at this point. You, as the project manager, will need to coordinate many people and processes at the same time, which can be challenging, especially if the project team members are actively involved in other, primary business activities at your firm.

And now for the final three steps to launch.

8. **Test a prototype.** Key to dashboard implementation is your testing of the prototype.[1] Show the prototype to at least one person of each user type. Have them use the dashboard and get

their feedback by watching and asking. If you want the dashboard to be used in a meeting, get a focus group of users together. Now is the time to check whether the dashboard is actually usable to decision makers, *not* after the official big-scale launch! Be aware that in some cases, several tests and prototypes will be required to get the final product. In all of my projects, I've found it better to start with easy-to-use and easy-to-populate dashboards rather than with an advanced multi-functional application based on sophisticated and complex databases.

9. **Analyze the results and make necessary changes.** Track the health of dashboard functionality very closely and take the test reactions into account. Pay attention to any activity related to the dashboard that you have not foreseen—it will help you to better meet your users' needs. Especially important at this point is to identify any obstacles that may prevent users from getting the full benefits from the dashboards; these are often tiny little things that you did not foresee that can easily and cheaply be changed before the major dashboard launch.

10. **Launch the dashboard in your organization.** This stage again involves several simultaneous tasks, and multiple departments (marketing, IT, finance, human resources, etc.) and thus it requires a good command of organizational skills. As a result, the project launch can be complex and time-consuming; however, effective management and communication will facilitate an excellent execution.

Further, once the project has been launched, you should not forget that the main purpose of any dashboard application is to lead to an action that will enhance the business performance of your company. To facilitate such an action based on dashboard analysis, you should assign individual accountability for each metric tracked and give these individuals the authority and resources needed to drive a change. Moreover, dedicating a *full-time employee* to the dashboard maintenance and support, and tying this employee's incentives to embedding the dashboard in decision making, will accelerate dashboard adoption throughout an organization.

EXECUTION CHALLENGES

Dashboards can be very effective performance measurement tools, yet dashboard projects frequently encounter tough challenges along the way. The experience of a business communication provider (the subject of Chapter 7's case study "The Right Call #1") illustrates some of these implementation challenges.

CASE STUDY

THE RIGHT CALL #2:
Implementation Challenges

Despite careful development of its marketing analytics dashboard, the business communication firm of Chapter 7's case study faced several challenges in implementation. First, its employees were focused on organizing isolated events, such as trade shows, conferences, and meetings with interested business owners and purchasing managers. Many employees feared that integrated performance management would expose them to criticism and punishment, and might reduce their budgets. In response, the company showed how the marketing analytics dashboard would instead help employees do a better job, and get rewarded for it.

Second, the company operated in many countries that differed substantially in economic development, market saturation, culture, infrastructure, and marketing actions. Country executives accused HQ (and each other) of "not getting it" and believed their specific country's situation was unique. In response, the dashboard team involved country managers from the start in the dashboard development. They assured managers that a standard measurement system did not imply that everyone needed to perform the same marketing actions or even had to weigh each performance metric in the same way. They shared the results on differences and similarities among countries in which drivers matter most to performance. As a result, country managers felt more understood, and more confident sharing success and failure stories with similar countries.

Finally, people disagreed on the value of offline marketing versus online marketing. Specifically, many felt that only offline marketing built awareness, interest, and preference, and that online marketing was unfairly credited for exploiting this brand equity in demand generation. In response, the company showed how both marketing channels contributed through simple correlations—after which dashboard users felt more comfortable with the analytics-based insights on the size and timing of performance effects of these marketing actions.

In this section I point out some of the critical challenges you may face when implementing a dashboard. If managers know possible risks and issues that might arise within dashboard implementation, they are better prepared to deal with such issues and resolve them.

First, decision makers are unlikely to use the analytic dashboard if they feel uncomfortable with either the data inputs or the assumptions that drive the model under the hood. Too often, dashboard developers fail to ensure that the database, used as a primary data source to build the dashboard, portrays data that is most useful to the dashboard users. Therefore it's essential to take extra precautions in order to prevent any data errors or even downward fraud in the measurement of a company's performance.

Moreover, dashboard users should at least feel that the underlying choice of the metrics was rigorous and that the metrics are relevant to their jobs. A dashboard can provide a breadth of information at a glance, but relying too much on its metrics without properly understanding their context can distort a dashboard user's overall view of the company and its performance. Dashboard metrics should transparently reflect the quality of decisions and actions of the dashboard users. At the same time, the latter should not be allowed to manipulate the data either before or after it has been captured within the dashboard system.

Second, some dashboards foster short-term decision making: Managers identify a problem area and immediately take action to fix it without identifying how this action will affect a company's long-term performance. This frequent error is another challenge of dashboard implementation—to be more precise, its interpretation. Dashboard users should be aware of this risk. They should interpret the data displayed on a dashboard and act upon information provided by considering both *short- and long-term consequences.* Only in this way will the dashboard deliver expected results.

Third, a dashboard is much more valuable if it has been carefully designed for the specific organization. There are many styles and formats available, and the best approach for presenting them will vary across companies. Consulting firms and software vendors actively promote dashboards, so executives and owners of risk management and performance measurement systems should ensure that the dashboards being created for their company are developed using a careful filtering process that considers their needs and challenges rather than being driven by the capabilities of existing software. It's no wonder that decision makers feel unsatisfied with a dashboard trying to fit their round problems into square holes.

Fourth, maintaining *transparent communications* with all levels of employees is very important in dashboard implementation.[2] It serves as an effective strategy for ensuring that a dashboard leads to more effective decision making inside organizations. Transparency allows managers to identify key risk factors at the strategic-entity level as well as at lower levels to better understand the full array of business risks impacting their organization. Therefore it's important for a dashboard to contain not just financial measures, but the necessary nonfinancial measures, such as customer and employee satisfaction, supply chain efficiency, etc., as well. Finally, open communication with employees helps managers design a dashboard that reflects the big picture of the company's business in a dynamic and accurate way.

In sum, the real execution challenges are typically not the ones most popular in the business press: a lack of visual appeal or the wrong technology/software. Instead, we found the real problems of dashboard users to be more fundamental.

KEY IMPLEMENTATION SUCCESS FACTORS

The key success factors that dashboard project managers often tend to miss include the following[3]:

- **Dashboards should be useful.** Dashboard irrelevance and uselessness is the number one reason for a dashboard project failure. If a dashboard is not designed to be user-friendly and contain information that fosters situation analysis and leads to action, it will not be adopted throughout your organization.

- **Dashboards should be aligned with strategy.** We have already discussed the importance of the alignment between the dashboard and the organization's strategy in Chapter 3. Dashboards misaligned with a company's strategy are doomed to fail.

- **Dashboards should contain the right metrics.** Boiling down an organization's vast array of metrics to a small and deliberate number of KPIs is almost always more difficult than most people realize. However, the metrics that your dashboard contains is the core of your entire project and thus essential to its success.

- **Dashboards should be clear and easy-to-read.** You may think of your dashboard implementation as a website project: You will have only a few seconds to capture somebody's attention and get your message across in the most powerful, efficient, and memorable manner possible. Good websites are not designed by accident—it takes time to draft and flesh out your communication and creative plans, layouts, content and storyboards, etc. The same challenges exist with dashboard projects. As a matter of fact, data visualization is probably one of the most misused and misunderstood forms of communications in the business world today. Slick and stunning data visualizations are useless if they are not used effectively, accurately, and in a highly deliberate manner.

- **Dashboards should be well planned.** Not a single one of the key success factors listed above could take place without good planning.

> **Dashboards require effective execution and committed people.** Dashboard projects often fail because people underestimate the effort required to implement them, and the employees who build dashboards often find themselves having a hard time managing the constantly changing scope and high expectations. Data visualization is unfamiliar or poorly understood. Project timelines get delayed, and momentum, excitement, and funding fizzle. Even highly motivated employees get sucked into big, messy, drawn-out projects, and all too often initiatives get canned even before the first dashboards appear.

> **Dashboard projects do not finish.** Useful, meaningful, and effective dashboards can be considered ongoing works-in-progress. Since good dashboards link strategy with execution, and since organizational strategies—along with their respective KPIs—change all the time, dashboards need to be updated regularly to stay relevant and concise. Therefore, successful dashboard projects do not end; instead, they are regularly updated, revised, and refined. Furthermore, dashboard projects are necessarily iterative. You should budget for a bunch of different versions in your project plan, and build the review process into your timelines, as you will likely have several iterations before your dashboards are deployed, from initial review to quality control to user-acceptance testing, so plan for them and expect changes to come. Experience will help you avoid derailing your project with every stakeholder review, but there is simply no way to avoid change.

Break your dashboard projects down into manageable phases, where each phase is relatively self-contained (individual functional areas, for example, sales, marketing, finance, etc.) and where the data required within each phase does not require a daunting amount of alignment and consolidation. You may also break down the dashboards aimed to serve different departments of your organization. This will help you deal with major dashboard implementation challenges.

In fact, executive satisfaction will be low if a complete dashboard is promised within a single project phase. The phase will take too much time and requirements will be incomplete as further considerations become apparent after the initial cockpit is delivered. Rather than setting expectations too high and failing to deliver, plan the project to include several iterative phases. This reduces the elapsed time and allows forward movement despite changing requirements.

In addition, deliver each phase rapidly in order to constantly demonstrate value and create opportunities to adjust your design philosophies and best practices with each successive rollout.

It is also critical that you bring the right stakeholders to your dashboard review meetings. However, it doesn't mean that there should be as many stakeholders as possible participating in your scoping and review sessions. In fact, the best organization-wide dashboard implementations are mostly run by a few key project participants who have insight into the entire initiative, from end to end. Different stakeholders from various functional areas might be required from phase to phase, but there should always be one or more key participants who have insight and experience with all of the phases.

Further, ad hoc research capabilities must be available, but they should be limited to solving exceptional situations. Common issues should be addressed by guided procedures that lead users to successful resolution consistently and efficiently through limited hyperlinks and simple question-and-answer dialogs. The development of these guided procedures identifies opportunities for process improvement. Focus research efforts where they earn the most value and enable new employees to climb the learning curve quickly. The guided procedure should go as far as necessary to ensure issue resolution.

Once an issue has been identified and researched, do not allow the knowledge gained to remain locked away in a chain of emails. Provide documentation facilities that attach narrative explanations directly to the dashboard results. Be certain these explanations are—and remain—

accessible to all users. This information also supports future business planning.

As we have already mentioned, requirements will change throughout the project, and indefinitely into the future. Therefore, use a technological backbone that facilitates adaptability. Provide administrative users the ability to maintain these relationships themselves.

Dashboard projects will be judged either as complete successes or complete failures. Tip the scales in your favor by engaging strong executive participation and maintaining ongoing interest through aggressive, iterative realization of a technically flexible solution. With an effective dashboard, organizations can fly safely and efficiently to their strategic destinations.

RENEWING THE MARKETING ANALYTICS DASHBOARD

Just as user feedback is crucial to successful dashboard implementation, it also naturally feeds into the renewal of the marketing analytics dashboard. Beyond the first three to six months of launch and (hopefully) honeymoon period, users will start to suggest specific changes to the dashboard to increase its value to them and update it to match changing conditions. Of particular concern are dashboard metrics that do not lead to sufficient insight or action, and important metrics that appear to be missing from the analytics dashboard. Indeed, the primary criterion for continued inclusion of a metric is the combination of *insight* and *action*. Insight derives from understanding the relation between specific actions and performance (typically in the past), suggesting new actions. Action implements what needs to be done to realize the potential benefits of the insight.

You may feel exhausted after careful dashboard design and launch, but it's important to treat the dashboard as a living document by actively seeking suggestions from users. Building in a function that makes it easy for users to make comments directly in the dashboard is an excellent way to solicit such input.

User input will signal the need for renewal. Several companies I helped years ago are still using the same dashboard, as the marketing responsiveness and sales conversion of key performance drivers has hardly changed. The analytic model remains the same, but is re-estimated every month with incoming data to keep the what-if analyses as current as possible. Other companies required minor changes to the dashboard, such as broadening data access to more users, or changing metric display priorities as markets matured and/or became more competitive. In most cases, though, there was a need for major renewal, such as changing the dashboard structure or adding/deleting KLPIs. While the dashboard may be "your baby," you need to be willing to remove metrics that do not drive specific insights to users. Moreover, ever-changing company strategies require reconsidering the alignment between the dashboard and the new goals at different levels in the organizational hierarchy.

Based on several case studies and surveys, here are seven tips for dashboard renewal:

1. Improve the measurement quality, especially for long-term market assets (such as brand equity).

2. Improve econometric models for what-if forecasts.

3. Ensure other stakeholders (finance, human resources) accept the marketing metrics.

4. Prioritize metrics in different periods (e.g., savings in recessions and growth in boom times).

5. Eliminate metrics that failed to drive specific insights or actions.

6. Develop new metrics for innovative marketing.

7. Give employees the incentive to show leadership in these new metrics.

WRAP-UP AND MANAGER'S MEMO

Just as any great strategy requires excellent execution, so does the best dashboard design need careful implementation. We summarized the essence of previous chapters in seven steps and added three launch steps to complete our checklist. Adding the challenges of execution and renewal leads us to the following twelve steps for dashboard implementation.

MANAGER'S MEMO

TWELVE STEPS TOWARD DASHBOARD IMPLEMENTATION

1. Communicate the dashboard initiative and get managerial and employee support.

2. Identify the project team.

3. Define the dashboard project scope.

4. Establish the data measurement system.

5. Gather requirements and candidate metrics.

6. Select and define KLPIs.

7. Design and construct a prototype.

8. Test the prototype with users.

9. Analyze the results and make necessary changes.

10. Launch the dashboard in your organization.

11. Anticipate and react to execution challenges.

12. Actively encourage user input to signal the need for dashboard renewal.

CHAPTER 13

Change Your Decision Making: From Interpretation to Action

Information is not knowledge. The only source of knowledge is experience.

—ALBERT EINSTEIN

The best business decisions come from intuitions and insights informed by data. Using data in this way allows your organization to build institutional knowledge and creativity on top of a solid foundation of data-driven insights.   —BLADT AND FILBIN, DOSOMETHING.ORG, 2013

AT THIS POINT IN OUR JOURNEY, you have to take an important leap of faith: from interpreting dashboard results to taking action based on the insights. In the words of one of the managers I worked with: "Lots of data and lots of action, but no link between the two." After all, if you or your organization does not change any decision based on dashboard insights, where is the incremental return on investment? Leading companies made millions by *acting* on their interpretation of analytics results. A key example in durables is Samsung, who in 2000 reallocated its marketing budget from North America and Russia to Europe and China and from air conditioning units and vacuum cleaners to LCD monitors and TVs. Within just two years, Samsung's brand value increased 30 percent, revenues increased from $27.7 to $34.7 billion, net income grew from $5.1 to $6 billion, and market share in LCD monitors and TVs went from eighth to second. A good example in fast-moving consumer goods is Heinz, who reallocated promotional spending across U.S. regions, cut spending by 40 percent, and increased market share by three points at the same time.

In fact, many managers and organizations are reluctant to change, despite all the enthusiasm about investment in the data, analytics, and dashboard journey. Risk aversion is part of this reluctance, but so is uncertainty about how company gains will benefit the individual decision maker—and who will be blamed if things go wrong. As one manager told us: "Look, I believe your metrics and your model: The company will most likely save $80M by cutting advertising spending. However, I will not see one cent of these savings. Moreover, if anything happens to go south and we lose 1 percent market share, I will be fired for cutting advertising." How much money is wasted and how many promising opportunities are not pursued in your company because of similar reasoning? Of course, consensus on dashboard metrics and compensation schemes can alleviate part of this issue. But senior leadership must also "walk the walk" by insisting on sound data and analysis to justify changing or maintaining the status quo and by demonstrating how to act based on the insights. As Harrah's entertainment CEO Gary Loveman put it: "There are two ways to get fired from Harrah's: stealing from the company, or failing to include a proper control group in your business experiment."[1]

Which practical steps can you take to help your organization move from insight to action? Experience and academic research points to four key steps.

1. **ADAPT** the dashboard output to the needs and decision-making style of the user.
2. **DECIDE** on rules for setting marketing budget and allocation.
3. **DESIGN** a (field) experiment to compare marketplace results of proposed action versus the status quo.
4. **ADDRESS** implementation challenges.

Let's look at these elements—with an easy mnemonic, ADDA—one by one.

ADAPT THE DASHBOARD OUTPUT

Decades of research in decision support systems have shown the importance of the fit between supply and demand in the adoption of a new decision aid. Each organization has a prevailing attitude and standard approach to doing things and making decisions. If your company has an outspoken analytical approach, exact numbers and caveats may be the desired input to decisions. On the other hand, if your company has a more intuitive or heuristic approach, visualizations should reflect this style. For instance, to compare the likely profit results of different combinations of two marketing actions, we built the heat map shown in Figure 13–1, which we discussed briefly in the case study "Cars: From Begging HQ to Talking Trade-Offs" in Chapter 1. (You will find it in color on my website, notthesizeofthedata.com).

The user builds a table combining two key decision variables, in this case price and TV advertising spending. Based on the model, the heat map shows the projected profit from each combination, indicating the higher profits in shades of green and the lower profits in shades of red. Here, they are shown in shades of gray, with the darker gray showing the greater profit. Note that the heat map does not restrict our decision options. Yes, one combination shows the highest projected profit, indicated in bold, but many other combinations imply better profits than the status quo (I've shown those in italics). For instance, if the organization feels uncomfortable raising the price beyond $40, it can obtain the highest profits with a TV ad budget of $3,500. Likewise, if the decision maker can only secure a budget of $2,000 for TV ads, the corresponding row in the heat map shows the highest attainable profit and the suggested price. Such restrictions could in principle be built into the model, but they tend to change rather fast in some organizations. Most often, it is left up to the decision maker at the time of the decision to evaluate such factors.

Figure 13–1, Heat Map of the Interaction of Two Marketing Variables on Profits

TV advertising in thousands of $	Price in $ 10	15	20	25	30	35	40	45	50	55	60	65	70	75
0	0.02	1.04	1.92	2.64	3.22	3.65	3.93	4.06	4.04	3.87	3.56	3.09	2.47	1.71
250	0.65	1.68	2.56	3.28	3.86	4.29	4.57	4.70	4.68	4.51	4.19	3.73	3.11	2.35
500	1.25	2.27	3.15	3.87	4.45	4.88	5.16	5.29	5.27	5.10	4.79	4.32	3.70	2.94
750	1.79	2.81	3.69	4.41	4.99	5.42	5.70	5.83	5.81	5.64	5.33	4.86	4.24	3.48
1000	2.28	3.30	4.18	4.91	5.48	5.91	6.19	6.32	6.30	6.13	5.82	5.35	4.73	3.97
1250	2.72	3.74	4.62	5.35	5.92	6.35	6.63	6.76	6.74	6.58	6.26	5.79	5.18	4.41
1500	3.11	4.13	5.01	5.74	6.32	6.74	7.02	7.15	7.13	6.97	6.65	6.18	5.57	4.80
1750	3.45	4.48	5.35	6.08	6.66	7.09	7.37	7.50	7.48	7.31	6.99	6.52	5.91	5.14
2000	3.74	4.77	5.65	6.37	6.95	7.38	7.66	7.79	7.77	7.60	7.28	6.82	6.20	5.44
2250	3.99	5.01	5.89	6.62	7.19	7.62	7.90	8.03	8.01	7.84	7.53	7.06	6.44	5.68
2500	4.18	5.21	6.08	6.81	7.39	7.81	8.09	8.22	8.21	8.04	7.72	7.25	6.64	5.87
2750	4.32	5.35	6.23	6.95	7.53	7.96	8.24	8.37	8.35	8.18	7.86	7.40	6.78	6.02
3000	4.42	5.44	6.32	7.05	7.62	8.05	8.33	8.46	8.44	8.27	7.96	7.49	6.88	6.11
3250	4.46	5.49	6.36	7.09	7.67	8.10	8.38	8.51	8.49	8.32	8.00	7.54	6.92	6.15
3500	4.46	5.48	6.36	7.09	7.66	8.09	8.37	8.50	8.48	8.31	8.00	7.53	6.91	6.15
3750	4.40	5.43	6.30	7.03	7.61	8.04	8.32	8.45	8.43	8.26	7.94	7.48	6.86	6.09
4000	4.30	5.32	6.20	6.93	7.50	7.93	8.21	8.34	8.32	8.15	7.84	7.37	6.75	5.99
4250	4.14	5.17	6.04	6.77	7.35	7.78	8.06	8.19	8.17	8.00	7.68	7.22	6.60	5.84
4500	3.94	4.97	5.84	6.57	7.15	7.57	7.85	7.98	7.97	7.80	7.48	7.01	6.40	5.63
4750	3.69	4.71	5.59	6.32	6.89	7.32	7.60	7.73	7.71	7.54	7.23	6.76	6.14	5.38
5000	3.38	4.41	5.29	6.01	6.59	7.02	7.30	7.43	7.41	7.24	6.92	6.46	5.84	5.08

The decision maker can also use the heat map to argue against proposals the model projects will reduce profits. In this case, dropping the price to $20 is only beneficial when the TV ad budget is at least doubled. Likewise, diminishing returns to TV ad spending imply that budgets of $4,000 are a waste of money. The heat map thus enables the user to get model input, but does not take away the human insights and power to actually make the decision.

More analytical decision makers may enjoy a tool like the slide bar example in Figure 13–2.

The slide bars allow us to display many decision variables at the same time, and allow the user to investigate the projected profit impact of small and large changes. For this durable goods manufacturer, profit is driven by the age of the product on the market, the price, the distribution share, and the budgets spent on TV and online ads. Foreign HQ's demands that management improve next-year profits from 4.45 to 5 (units scaled for confidentiality), while no product updates are provided and the product age on the market thus will increase from twelve to twenty-four months. Management used the slide bar tool to communicate to headquarters that profits would instead go down to 3.32, unless more advertising budgets were provided (price and distribution share were considered stable). In this case, increasing the TV ad budget from $500,000 to $1.38M would suffice to bring profits up to the tar-

Figure 13–2, Slide Bars for Manipulating Marketing Variables

Change the levels of the marketing variables to see how the profits change.

Profits	4.775

Marketing Variables

Slide Bars		
Product age (months)	12.00	◀ ▶
Price	15.00	◀ ▶
TV ads	2,005	◀ ▶
Online ads	200	◀ ▶
Distribution share	20	◀ ▶

get level of 5. In this case, use of the scroll bar tool not only led to a more productive discussion on the specific budget for the coming year, but also stimulated a larger debate on the company's product development cycles, profit targets, and marketing investments.

Both the heat map and the slide bar tool focus on decisions with a long time horizon, such as yearly budget setting. More useful for tactical planning are tools that display more detailed timing of actions and results. For example, the dashboard shown in Figure 13–3 is used by the furniture seller to make daily investments in Google AdWords, flyers, faxes, and price discounts. This dashboard should look familiar by now; you met it in Chapter 1, and again in the case study "The Right Chair #2" in Chapter 11.

In this dashboard, the user can change any of the marketing actions and observe the project profit impact over time. This is important when marketing actions have vastly different wear-in times (e.g., discounts work directly, but flyers take many periods before resulting in a sale). Moreover, the decision maker may care about obtaining results at specific times, such as reaching quotas by quarter's end.

Figure 13–3, Inofec Dashboard

Period	Flyers	Faxes	Adwords	Discount
1	0	400	100	7
2	0	0	50	7
3	0	0	50	7
4	4000	0	100	7
5	0	0	100	7
6	0	0	100	7
7	0	400	100	7
8	0	0	100	7
9	0	0	50	7
10	0	0	50	7
11	4000	0	100	7
12	0	0	100	7
13	0	0	100	7
14	0	0	100	7

Total Profits: $333,068.88

DECIDE ON RULES FOR SETTING MARKETING BUDGET AND ALLOCATION

To optimize or not to optimize? Just the allocation of the budget or also its size? These are key questions to address when moving from interpretation to action. The answer may seem clear to some: "Of course, we should optimize everything!" However, this requires a lot of confidence in the assumptions of the model and in the belief that the (near) future will be like the past. "Optimal" recommendations don't help you if no decision maker would implement them. Table 13–1 gives an overview of your options.

Table 13–1, Optimizing and Adjusting Budget Allocation and Size

	Budget Allocation Only	Budget Size and Allocation
Optimize	Ratio of elasticities	Rules for optimizing budget
	Case: online retailer	Case 1: Constant ad–sales effect
		Case 2: Constant % ad–sales effect
Adjust	Shift allocation in recommended direction	Shift size and allocation in recommended direction
	Case: furniture marketer	Case: Inofec

Optimize Budget Allocation

Starting with the top left in Table 13–1, the *golden rule of allocation optimization* is the ratio of elasticities. If doubling your budget on offline advertising increases your sales by 10 percent (elasticity = 10%÷100% = 0.1) while doubling your budget on online advertising increases your sales by 20 percent (elasticity = 0.2), you should spend two-thirds of your budget on online advertising. Sounds intuitive, right? Let's see how this works *in practice*, in the following case study of the European online retailer we met in Chapter 9, based on the work by De Haan, Wiesel, and myself.

ONLINE MARKETING EFFECTS
Shifting Euros Away from Last-Click Misattribution

In the Fall of 2011, managers of a large European online retailer needed help. They are responsible for each of five very different product categories: Fashion, Electronics, Entertainment & Hardware, Home & Gardening, Sports & Leisure, and Beauty & Wellness. All of the company's sales occur online, and managers were specifically interested in the effectiveness of their seven online paid marketing activities: (1) emails, (2) search engine advertising (SEA) for the retailer itself, (3) SEA for specific products, (4) retargeting, (5) portal websites advertising, (6) affiliates website advertising, and (7) comparison website.

At the time, the retailer favors product-related SEA (one-third of its online paid marketing budget), which managers intuitively believed was effective. However, they checked this intuition with two attribution methods: last-click based on the same session (which is the last paid advertising the consumer clicked on before purchase?) and based on the last seven days (which paid advertising did the consumer click on in the full week before purchase?). These last-click models suggested to only allocate 10 percent (same-session method) or 12 percent (seven-days method) of the marketing budget to product-related SEA. Instead, emails should get the lion's share of the budget (44 percent). The retail managers were highly suspicious of these results, but did not have any evidence to back them up. For the time being, they adjusted the last-click recommendations on their own judgment and optimize it using trial and error. However, they knew they needed better ways to allocate their budgets.

Two colleagues and I went to work with daily data on online advertising spending and sales performance, using a structural version[2] of the vector autoregressive model (SVAR) detailed in Chapter 8. The long-term advertising-sales elasticities are shown in Figure 13–4.

Across all categories, the retailer got most bang for its buck for advertising on third-party websites, then for SEA and retargeting, and finally for emails. The exact ranking within third-party websites changed with the category: for example, affiliate websites and comparison websites dominated for Fashion, Electronics, and Entertainment & Hardware;

Figure 13–4, Long-Term Sales Percentage Increase from a 100 Percent Increase in Online Advertising

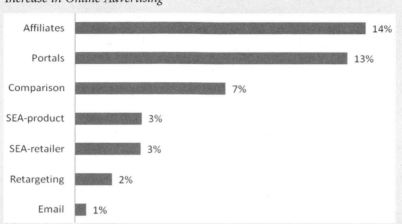

while portals were key for Home & Gardening and Sports & Leisure Affiliates, and comparison sites for Beauty & Wellness. After review, managers agreed that these elasticities made sense, while adding new insights as they differed from both plain intuition and the last-click methods.

How do these findings translate into a proposed budget allocation? The proposed SVAR allocation in Figure 13–5, which uses the *ratio of elasticities*, contrasts with both the current allocation and last-click methods.

Management intuition was vindicated in the low effectiveness we found for emails. However, the SVAR recommendations for search-engine advertising and retargeting were closer to the last-click attribution methods. Most important, the SVAR results consistently recommended spending a lot more on third-party websites (affiliates, portals, and price comparison sites). Thus, management intuition was correct in adjusting the last-click method suggestions upward for third-party websites, but did not go far enough. The quantitative results emboldened them to go where they had never gone before in terms of spending on portals, affiliates, and comparison sites. The SVAR model also projected that executing the proposed allocation would raise company revenues by 17 percent over the current allocation (and 62 percent over the allocation suggested by the last-click method) without increasing the marketing budget. But would you be enthusiastic about implementing the proposed allocation?

Figure 13–5, Current Allocation vs. Proposed (SVAR) and Last-Click Attribution Models

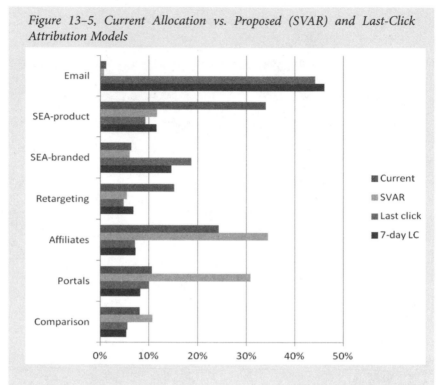

It all depends on your faith in a few assumptions. First, the proposed allocation differs rather dramatically from the current one. Maybe portals had a high effectiveness at 11 percent budget, but that does not guarantee their effectiveness at 31 percent. The model did account for diminishing returns, but depends on the limited variation in past data to estimate such diminishing returns. No matter how complete and brilliant the model is, it can never account for everything that might possibly go wrong.

Second, you need to have faith that the (near) future will be like the (near) past. In this specific project, no data was available on competitive advertising, thus its effect on the companies own revenues could not be modeled. If competitive pressure remains similar in the near future, this does not represent a big problem. The same goes for other potential revenue drivers such as the economy, regulation, the weather, etc. The point is, the manager may know about such changes, and this knowledge should be part of the decision, even if it is not in the model.

Adjust Budget Allocation

What can you do if you hesitate to apply the proposed allocation because you don't believe in key assumptions or have other reasons? What human beings have been doing for thousands of years: *Adjust gradually toward the proposed optimal solution!* Moving to the bottom left corner of two-by-two Table 13–1, why not gradually shift your allocation in the direction of the proposed one? You can then observe the results in the marketplace and adjust when necessary. A key example is the experience of Inofec, the office furniture seller in the Netherlands (discussed in the case study "The Right Chair #2" in Chapter 6). Based on the vector autoregressive model explained in Chapter 8, I calculated both the profit increase of a 1 euro increase in an advertising activity, and the advertising-sales elasticity (the percentage increase in sales from a 1 percent increase in advertising spending). The results for the three advertising actions—faxes, flyers (direct mail), and Google AdWords (paid search ads)—are shown in Table 13–2.

Table 13–2, Profit Effects and Sales Elasticities for Inofec Furniture

	Profit Effect of 1 € Increase	Sales Elasticity
Fax	3.33	0.05
Flyers	0.57	0.04
AdWords	55.72	4.35

The company was shocked to find out that flyers, representing 80 percent of its marketing spend, gave back only 0.57 for every euro spent! In contrast, Google AdWords (13 percent of the budget) gave back 100 times as much for every euro spent. The "ratio of elasticities" rule would have had us take the last column of Table 13–2 and recommend spending 98 percent of the budget on AdWords, which obviously was uncomfortable both for me and for the company. After discussing the findings, we agreed instead to double the AdWords

Table 13–3, Net Profit Changes for 3 Months During vs. 3 Months Before Field Experiment

	Base AdWords	Double AdWords
Base flyers	1	7.5
Half flyers	12.5	14.2

budget and to cut the flyers budget by half in a field experiment. For four matched regions, the experiment ran for three months (June–August 2009) with a base (no changes in the planned flyer campaigns) and low condition for flyer spending and a base and high condition for AdWords spending. We agreed to evaluate for each region the change in net profit (revenues – cost of goods sold – marketing expenses) compared to the same region's past profits. The results of this two-by-two experiment are shown in Table 13–3, with profit increases in the base condition (same flyer and AdWords allocation) set to 1.

First, the field experiment supports our recommendations: doubling AdWords and halving flyers yields a profit increase 14.2 times larger than in the control condition! Second, the cost savings from cutting flyers are even more impressive than the extra revenues from doubling AdWords. Third, we reestimated the model with the data during the experiment to check whether the estimated elasticities still hold. They did, except for the condition with base AdWords and halved flyers. In that condition, the elasticity of the remaining flyers became considerably higher, indicating it was not a good idea to cut flyers further. Apparently, flyers themselves were a fine marketing tool, the company had just been spending way past the point of diminishing returns. Indeed, a key lesson for Inofec's management was resisting the temptation to simply boost flyer spending whenever they suspected demand might start to soften (as they had in the past). Instead, "shoot-first" reactions were replaced by a spreadsheet-driven dashboard tool that allowed decision makers to compare alternative marketing plans to address market challenges. As the founder explained: "We are going to

Figure 13–6, Sales Increase from an Increase in Marketing Spending

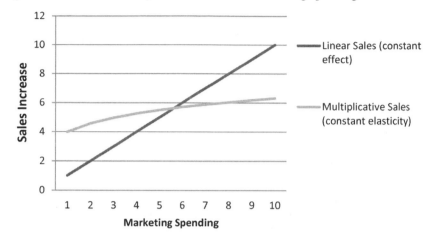

design way more elaborate marketing strategies. In doing so, we will focus on the linkages between online and offline activities, explicitly distinguish the effects, and explore new opportunities due to new technical developments."[3]

Optimize Budget Size

Moving from budget allocation to budget size, additional assumptions are needed for optimization. Especially important is the shape of the effect of marketing on sales. While this may be highly complex, our experience shows you can get close enough with either (1) a linear effect (same sales increase for each dollar spent on marketing) or (2) a multiplicative effect (same sales percentage increase for each percentage of increase in marketing spend). The difference is shown in Figure 13–6.

Let's look at these two effects more closely. In the linear effect scenario, you get approximately the same sales increase for each dollar spent more on marketing. In the multiplicative effect scenario, you get less and less for each dollar spent. This is known as diminishing returns. Of course, your effect shape only needs to apply in a certain range, the range in which you are making decisions. For instance, if you would never consider spending less than $10,000 (because you believe that is not enough to break through the clutter and have any sales effect), it's not important how the sales effect behaves under $10,000. Indeed, we almost never observe the intuitive S-shaped effect curve (increasing returns below a threshold, diminishing returns above a threshold) in the marketplace because managers know better than to spend below the minimal threshold.

Dorfman and Steiner set the budget! If your effect of marketing on sales size is *linear*, how large should your budget be? This problem was solved in 1954 by economists Dorfman and Steiner.[4] Here is their optimal budget-setting rule:

Advertising / sales revenues ratio = ad elasticity / price elasticity

For instance, if ad elasticity = 0.2 and price elasticity = −2, you should spend 10 percent of your sales revenues on advertising. And when the situation changes, you should change your spending. The more effective your advertising becomes (higher elasticity), the more you should spend on advertising. The more price-sensitive your market becomes (which reduces the price and thus the margin you can obtain), the less money you make on each sale, and thus the less you should advertise.

While the Dorfman/Steiner formula above is elegant and widely used in academia, managers have been hesitant to apply it to their own company. One key issue is that managers don't know advertising and price elasticities. Instead, many companies use the advertising-to-sales ratio in their industry as a benchmark for their own spending. This is not wrong if all competitors have similar advertising and price elasticities as you do. Most often, they don't: your product and positioning may face lower/higher price sensitivity—so a high-end player should advertise more than a low-end player. Likewise, your advertising effectiveness may be twice as high as that of the competition, in which case you should advertise twice as much.

The Wright rule rules! Another key issue is that the advertising-to-sales effect may not be linear, but *multiplicative*. Increasing your ad budget from $1M to $2M (+100 percent) may increase sales from $10M to $11M (+10 percent), but to achieve the next 10 percent sales increase, you may need to further double the ad budget from $2M to $4M, instead of simply adding another $1M to it. Such a multiplicative relationship is implicit in the most common models for demand estimation. In that case, we have the Wright rule,[5] which shows that the optimal budget-setting rule now is:

$$\text{Optimal ad spending} = \text{Gross contribution x ad elasticity}$$
$$= \text{Unit contribution x expected sales x ad elasticity}$$

In words, managers should set their advertising budget to be equal to advertising elasticity times gross profit. In the absence of better information, they can assume that advertising elasticity is 0.10 and spend 10 percent of gross profit on advertising. This budgeting rule is simple enough to be applied by any business that knows its gross profit, including small and medium enterprises.

Change is the only constant! What are the marketing implications when conditions change? First, the more contribution per product, the more you should advertise. Second, the higher your ad elasticity, the more you should advertise. Note that both implications also follow from the Dorfman-Steiner rule. Third, the higher expected sales, the more you should advertise. For instance, suppose you expect a pending recession, which will reduce demand for your product. At the same time, your unit contribution will not increase and may even decrease. The Wright rule states that you should *cut advertising budget unless* your advertising elasticity increases substantially! Your advertising elasticity may increase during a recession because competitors cut back on their advertising, enabling you to obtain cheaper media buys and to obtain higher response to your ads from customers. In fast-moving consumer goods, advertising elasticities are twice as high under low competitive clutter versus high competitive clutter.[6]

How should your advertising budget change over time for a new product? In the U.S. car market, advertising elasticities are nine times higher when companies have a substantially new product.[7] In other markets, the average advertising elasticity is 0.26 for new products (for three years after launch) and 0.05 otherwise. Therefore, the launch budget should be 26 percent of anticipated profit for the first years, and then should decrease to a 5 percent maintenance budget.

Despite its appeal, Wright's rule also encounters several objections. Most important: How can you determine "expected sales" to plug into the equation, if sales depend on your advertising spending? Moreover, managers still need to estimate the advertising elasticity.

One key practical objection to any of the optimal rules is that they assume profit maximization is the only firm objective. For instance, while implementing optimal price and promotion policies at BauMax, managers realized that, while profits indeed increased, sales decreased.[8] This observation entailed emotional discussions with merchandise managers, who were afraid of missing their sales and volume targets and felt the need to defend their market shares. Moreover, the purchasing department liked huge sales because it allowed quantity discounts from suppliers. After careful debate, it was decided that profit would have a weight of 70 percent in the optimization exercise.

Adjust Budget Size

How about *directionally* changing toward the optimal budget size? As implemented in the heat map and slide bars in this chapter, we can show decision makers the projected performance for a wide range of budget size. In the heat map example, directionally increasing the TV budget was clearly feasible, even though the optimal budget size could not be attained due to funding restrictions. The slide bars offered profit projections for the smallest changes to the budget.

Practical applications of directionally changing budgets abound in

"Practice Prize" papers on operations (Zara) and marketing (Bayer and BauMax). In Zara's case, some managers decided to overrule the recommendations, which provided a wonderful test and convinced managers that the calculated optimal strategy was better. In BauMax's case, managers used a phased roll-out as a low-risk strategy of initial model implementation. They started with a limited number of articles in ten representative Austrian test stores. Sales and profit performance of these articles was then benchmarked against a group of reference stores with similar characteristics to the test outlets. Next, the optimal strategy was extended to more articles and to other countries. As the BauMax CFO and CIO put it: "We were not sure whether we can rely on a computer program that takes over decisions that are in the core of our business. Hence, benchmarking has always been a central issue. We wanted to know exactly what the impact of any change was, and we wanted to interfere if things went wrong."[9]

ADDRESSING IMPLEMENTATION CHALLENGES

Implementation of any allocation and budget size rules uncovers additional challenges that need to be addressed. In BauMax's case, an approval work-flow tool provided excellent feedback for both fine-tuning the decision support system and improving communication between users and the project development group. Most user rejections of project recommendations were caused by expectations that larger package sizes had to be more expensive, but that the same product in different colors had to be priced the same—independent of different company margins. Users insisted on maintaining product line size parities for such product families and as a consequence the model had to be adjusted.

While these differ from case to case, we also see common themes in the seven years of INFORMS Practice Prize, spanning four continents and industries as diverse as automotive, consumer packaged goods, catalog sales, durables, airlines, insurance, and telecommunications.[10] These common implementation challenges relate to:

➢ Executives' time.

➢ Interdepartmental coordination.

➢ Data integration and management.

➢ Showing that implementation pays for itself.

➢ Trust.

In firms like Bayer and Whirlpool, the lack of executives' time was a significant barrier to changing the mental models. At the Allstate insurance company, a strategic project required the approval and involvement of the finance and accounting departments. Because marketing was in disfavor before the new CMO took over, any major marketing investment required strong buy-in from the financial controller. At Inofec, most of the project's time was spent on data integration and management, for which a new person had to be hired. At Chrysler, "with just this one test they made more than they paid for the project."[11] Finally, trust is essential as not all decision makers have full understanding of the model behind the recommendations. At Campbell's, "the firm does not need to look under the bonnet. They just need to trust the people that do."[12]

Trust is also a key factor from the broader experience with decision support systems, which lists three implementation success factors: trust, expectations, and attitude:

1. **Trust.** Decision makers should trust the metrics in the marketing dashboard. They should trust that the numbers are correct and not manipulated. Also, they should not have the impression that the marketing dashboard is meant to monitor or control them; neither should they see the dashboard as an infringement on their professional autonomy.

2. **Expectations.** Management of expectations is key to successful implementation. If the expectations are low, there is little incentive for use. Setting expectations high will help to generate initial use of the market dashboard, but this may

backfire when the experience does not (immediately) live up to the expectations. In particular, users should be prepared for bugs and start-up problems when a market dashboard is just installed.

3. **Attitude.** The technology acceptance model (TAM) asserts that one of the main drivers of the attitude toward an information system is its "perceived usefulness."[13] Perceived usefulness refers to the extent to which a user believes that a specific system will enhance his/her job performance. Decision makers should be convinced that they do their job better when using the market dashboard.

In sum, your best chances at getting decision makers to take action based on dashboard insights involves generating trust in the dashboard metrics and recommendations, managing expectations to accurately reflect benefits and start-up problems, and ensuring decision makers that using the dashboard will make their job better.

WRAP-UP AND MANAGER'S MEMO

True knowledge comes only from experience, which requires acting on insights. However, such action requires communication, courage, and crossing the comfort threshold of the decision maker.

Our examples covered four continents and industries as diverse as automotive, consumer packaged goods, online retailers, catalog sales, durables, airlines, insurance, do-it-yourself chains, and telecommunications. In all cases, applying marketing analytics, insights, and action led to large, quantifiable lifts in company performance. For Inofec furniture, the analytics were incorporated into a dashboard adapted to the decision makers, which developed the confidence to make substantial shifts to marketing budget size and allocation. Profit increased fourteen-fold as a result. Such drastic profit increases are typical for smaller companies that first start using analytics. In larger companies, interdepartmental coordination makes such action often harder to get agreement and implementation. Still, the benefits are substantial and more than pay back for the project itself. (You can point doubters to the experience of companies such as AllState, Bayer, Campbell, Chrysler, and Whirlpool.)

Such case studies in your industry can help you get the internal buy-in to go ahead. Still, there is no substitute for applying analytics to your own data, developing your own insights, and taking the actions that will set you apart.

MANAGER'S MEMO

HOW TO TAKE ACTION IN FIVE STEPS

1. Adapt the dashboard output to the needs and decision-making style of the user.

2. Decide on rules for setting marketing budget and allocation.

3. Share relevant case studies on how companies similar to yours succeeded by taking action.

4. Design a (field) experiment to compare marketplace results of proposed action versus the status quo.

5. Address implementation challenges on the lack of executives' time, interdepartmental coordination, data integration, and trust.

CHAPTER 14

Nurturing the Culture and Practice of Accountability

The real revolution in data will be a change in organizational behavior and culture—and those changes are hard and take time. Many organizations will struggle with the shift, and frankly, many will be usurped by new competitors who grow up natively with this new worldview.

—SCOTT BINKER, CHIEF MARKETING TECHNOLOGIST, 2013

ORGANIZATIONAL CULTURE IS CRUCIAL TO DASHBOARD SUCCESS

Marketing analytics dashboards (MADs) are not culture-neutral. They require the spark of an organization that desires to market smarter, and they create a fire that purifies and further flames this desire. In our experience, certain cultural factors provide an ideal breeding ground for the MAD idea:

- The perceived need to manage by exception (MBE), often fueled by information overload.
- The desire to focus the firm on targeted metrics that both reflect and affect performance.
- A crisis that makes many employees realize the need for change and accountability.

> ➤ Higher expectations for marketing due to mergers or expansions in different countries, industries, or channels.

Don't underestimate the potential of analytics dashboards: Data-driven decision making can transform your company into a performance-accountable organization. At the same time, however, don't underestimate the cultural and political challenges. An organization becomes performance-accountable when management commits to increasing each employee's knowledge and understanding of what drives business performance of the company. A dashboard implies such a commitment from the very start of its implementation and therefore cultural modification is inevitable. Research across hundreds of senior executives revealed that a supportive analytics culture is crucial for the effective use of marketing analytics dashboards.[1] The people who perform marketing analytics can be different from those who implement the insights, but you need both groups to actively support the use of marketing analytics.

The dashboard's cultural impact on a company is embedded in its nature, its DNA. Dashboards allow individual employees to see the big picture and understand the impact of their actions on the rest of the company. Each employee is assigned a goal through a dashboard, uses the latter to understand the context of his/her role within the project/department/company, and further uses the dashboard to check his/her individual performance against that context. In this way, dashboards create the sense of accountability throughout an organization.

If implemented effectively, dashboards popularize an accountability culture, which becomes a main pillar of a company's corporate culture. Furthermore, dashboards enable executives to align resources, creating an organization that can respond quickly to change and further nurture a culture of transparency and accountability.

Organizations depend on multiple people and information sources to understand the state of the business, and therefore they are very often overloaded with information, which is frequently duplicate, incomplete, or inconsistent. Dashboards allow such organizations to move away from an information-overload environment. However, changes that dashboards bring require alignment of a company's business strategy. Such an alignment will then ensure accountability throughout an organization.

Dashboards drive a culture of transparency—and accountability—throughout the organization because they monitor progress toward achieving corporate, departmental, or individual goals. The beauty of this performance measurement tool is that employees at all levels, including those with little technical knowledge, can get the information they need in a timely manner without calling the IT help desk.

In this type of culture—transparent and accountable—managers have the opportunity to make their own decisions and act quickly based on the information they can access via their dashboard. Culture comes into play at the start of the dashboard project: Chapter 3 taught us a company must go through an initial discovery process to learn and evaluate the cultural changes that dashboards will have on its people as well as its business position. Culture also comes into play at the end of the process: To reap the full benefits of marketing analytic dashboards, companies must reassess what motivates employees and how to nudge them toward the practice of accountability.

MOTIVATING EMPLOYEES TO USE THE DASHBOARD

The big question of "what motivates employees?" plays the most critical role in such a process. Without a solid answer to this question, dashboards will be off target as tools to help employees do a better job. We have some basic recommendations to motivate employees to use the dashboard in their conversations and decisions:

- Explain the role of an employee in the dashboard project and his/her impact on the company's performance.
- Emphasize employee benefits: ability to track, adjust, improve, and show personal performance.

- ➤ Encourage a dashboard trial.
- ➤ Invite employee feedback and use it in the dashboard.
- ➤ Incorporate dashboards into day-to-day operations.
- ➤ Develop a performance-related incentive scheme.

Got your attention with the last recommendation? Because so much is at stake, many managers are reluctant to change the compensation structure. Of course in the initial phases of a dashboard implementation, you want to reward employees for providing the correct data and speaking the dashboard language. At two multinationals I worked with, country managers in the first year only needed to specify the metrics they were targeting (e.g., increase preference by 10 percent) and put the "before and after" measurements in place. However, once the data was analyzed and included in the marketing analytics dashboard, managers could now track not just whether a specific campaign was successful in moving that target metric, but also how much the target metrics in turn lifted sales. At that point, senior management felt it knew enough to start paying bonuses based on performance that exceeded the dashboard predictions.

If you are in doubt, consider these reasons for tying compensation to dashboards:[2]

- ➤ Dashboards quantify and qualify the activity-to-success ratios, creating a *straight connection* between employee behavior and incentives that directly impact individuals.
- ➤ Rather than prod employees to become more productive, many firms tie individual performance to incentives directly related to their compensation programs using dashboard metrics. It *beats more subjective evaluation* in empowerment and clarity.

In other words, if you design the compensation right, employees should *prefer* to use the dashboard as both a monitoring tool and a way to improve their own performance before the next review. If this sounds utopian, check out the experience of companies as different as Avaya, Harrah's, and Vanguard.[3] In each of these cases, the dashboard was accepted as an integral part of performance assessment throughout the company.

THE PRACTICE OF ACCOUNTABILITY

While the previous culture and employee motivation considerations are crucial to strategic success, the tactical benefits of dashboard use depend on stimulating and maintaining a practice of accountability. In this process, managers should keep three lessons in mind.

The first lesson is that it's imperative that managers and knowledge workers alike understand that *dashboards communicate interconnected metrics for action.* Otherwise, there is a danger that dashboards will become a dumping ground for incongruous, unrelated, unlinked data that are not tied to the overall business or are contextually irrelevant to an employee or functional unit.

The second lesson is that dashboards should help answer tough questions that organizations need to ask themselves, such as:

- What does each person in each functional area need to do to support the individual business goal?
- How does an individual perform the role that ultimately drives performance at the top line?
- Where is the connection between an employee's individual role and the overall success of the company?

And third, the company should decide on *breadth of data accessibility* that will drive each dashboard.

Answering these questions requires a fresh look at how employee activities relate to corporate goals. Often, employees have only the vaguest idea. This has driven much of the corporate work around performance measurement systems and tools. Marketing has been less engaged in this process. As a result, it witnesses both enthusiasm for the dashboard concept and patchy implementation in practice.

Marketing analytic dashboards, in particular, perform a number of accountability culture–related functions, such as:

- ➤ Helping to clarify and define the role of marketing in the company.
- ➤ Creating a learning organization that makes decisions based on hard facts supplemented with experiential intuition rather than lots of intuition punctuated by a few facts.
- ➤ Establishing clear roles and responsibilities, which create job satisfaction and a culture of performance and success.
- ➤ Elevating marketing accountability to earn the trust and confidence of the CEO, the CFO, and others throughout the company.

Overall, the practice of accountability is an everyday responsibility and requires commitment of all employees. It should be a big part of employees' business routine, guiding the way they think about the business their company is engaged in; without the active practice of accountability, dashboards can rarely succeed, as they heavily rely on adoption rate throughout an organization.

HOW TO SUPPORT ACCOUNTABILITY THROUGHOUT THE ORGANIZATION

Once the initial culture, employee motivation, and practice are in place, the issue is how to best support this accountability culture throughout an organization. How can you maintain the culture of transparency and accountability after dashboard project launch? Here are some suggestions regarding stimulation of dashboard usage, as a big part of an accountability culture and business performance system:

- ➤ Make the dashboard software a *part of the user computers*, and provide appropriate soft training (seminars, electronic presentations, etc.) for those who wish it.

- ➤ Enforce the dashboard as the corporate standard tool for viewing the business, for delivering critical messages to employees, and for completing individual performance evaluations.
- ➤ Tie dashboards to employees' incentives and thus encourage them to use dashboards on a regular basis in order to track their personal progress toward preestablished business objectives.

Culture is always difficult to change—in every sphere of life. In the context of dashboard implementation, senior management routines—how they allocate their time, prepare their agendas, and the information they consider are part of the firm's culture—are impervious to change, especially by outsiders. Paradoxically, in many large firms, the CMO is an outsider, and not in a position to change the way senior management sees the business. Therefore, it's especially difficult for a marketing department to initiate the cultural shift, grow loyalty to transparent and accountable culture, and cultivate the latter at all layers of the company.

Implementing a dashboard project is an ongoing daily responsibility. It requires a cultural shift toward adoption of measurement practices and a system in general that will support dashboards. A company's top management should be prepared for such a shift more than its knowledge workers. The firm's senior executives should effectively communicate the key message that "a measurement system is an everyday responsibility of every employee." The top managers should be the ones responsible for incremental injection of a measurement and a culture of accountability into employees' business routines. In other words, management should drive adoption of both dashboards and accountability culture throughout the organization.

Another factor that will positively impact an accountability culture adoption is dashboard standardization. Dashboard management means dealing with business performance data every day (or as frequently as possible or appropriate for a specific business) and sustaining dashboard projects on a regular basis. Frequent evaluation, analysis, and modification of dashboards will ultimately lead to standardization of dashboards. Once dashboard practices have been standardized, both effectiveness and efficiency of dashboard usage will be improved. Dashboard standardization will allow and result in quicker responses to factors that influence business performance of a company or its functional units.

Dashboard standardization, however, does not mean that dashboards should remain constant, quite the opposite—the dashboards should be regularly revisited and improved. Managers should keep in mind that dashboards are dynamic in nature and will constantly need an ongoing update and maintenance. Dashboard standardization will definitely make it easier to use, and will allow the dashboard to become a part of a company's business culture and practices. Do not, however, sacrifice its vibrancy and flexibility to the simplicity of standardization.

Finally, due to the challenges of dashboard implementation, the excitement and enthusiasm about its application often weaken and may ultimately fade away. In order to keep the dashboard project alive, its benefits should outweigh its costs. And these benefits must be communicated to the end users. However, verbal communication itself is not sufficient under these circumstances. The dashboard users should be motivated to use the application and support the accountability culture by very specific and clear means. Developing performance-related incentive schemes that will motivate an employee to keep track of his/her individual progress is probably the most effective method to foster the culture of accountability and facilitate a conscious choice of an employee to use a dashboard. On the management side, the fact that may influence dashboard adoption by senior executives is that the dashboard application is a very popular industry/market trend, and major high-performance companies have already adopted this innovation and demonstrated actual benefits of dashboard systems in place. Although this approach is not new, it is very effective when persuading top managers to go along with dashboard initiative and adopt an accountability culture within the firm, especially if the industry/market benchmarks are represented by the main competitors of the firm.

WRAP-UP AND MANAGER'S MEMO

We agree with chief marketing technologist Scott Binker that the real revolution in data and analytics will be change in organizational culture. You can't simply turn the switch—even with the best marketing analytic dashboard—and simply hope that decision makers will get on board. In this chapter, we reviewed why culture is crucial to dashboard success, how to motivate employees to use a dashboard, establish the practice of accountability, and maintain its culture over time.

How will you start tomorrow to make this happen? We leave you with these seven excellent pieces of advice from firms who recently went through the experience.[4]

MANAGER'S MEMO

SEVEN SUGGESTIONS FOR INSTILLING A CULTURE OF ACCOUNTABILITY

1. Above all, get started now! The learning curve is steep for marketing accountability, and your firm's satisfaction with the journey increases over time.

2. Ensure you are using some kind of metric for each of your marketing actions.

3. Be ready to invest in getting some data on these metrics.

4. Coordinate your traditional and digital media campaigns.

5. Set specific measurable objectives for all your campaigns.

6. Involve external vendors in dashboard goals—this helps them understand your expectations to retain them or to cut them loose.

7. Link dashboard-based performance to employee compensation, as a bonus.

CONCLUSION

Call to Action

You don't need software—you need courage and a vision.
—GAL BORENSTEIN, CEO OF THE BORENSTEIN GROUP, 2009

WE HAVE COME TO THE END OF THIS BOOK—but certainly not of our journey in marketing smarter. All of the advice, science, art, and case studies can help you prepare moving onward and upward, but there is no substitute for actually doing it. The world of marketing will not get any easier the longer we wait—starting now will find you more ready for the changes that lie ahead: Fortune favors the prepared!

I hope this book has made the journey clearer in your mind and the conviction firmer in your heart. Don't get discouraged with the gap between where you are and where you now know you could be. Don't get distracted with the latest flashy software, management fad, or smooth-talking vendor. You don't need the latest in fancy design—you need courage and a vision!

I wrote this book to serve you as a guide and a reference on this journey. Just as every chapter ended with a wrap-up, so too does this book. Chapter 1 showed what marketing analytics dashboards are, why your organization needs them, who in your organization can benefit from them, and how. A marketing analytics dashboard is a concise set of interconnected performance drivers to be viewed in common throughout the organization.

Chapter 2 helped you to assess your organization's current scorekeeping tools in these terms. Simple reporting dashboards do not link metrics to marketing actions, to each other, or to hard (often financial) performance. Balanced scorecards are often neither concise nor actionable. Marketing analytics dashboards both show the situation and help the user dig deeper for insights and inspiration for action.

Chapter 3 assisted you to formulate the vision and align marketing goals with business strategy objectives. Communicating this vision upward and sideways helps you to harness top management support and gain employee engagement.

Chapter 4 brought together the team for the dashboard project and gave concrete tips to manage the team and productively resolve the typical conflicts.

Chapter 5 focused on a crucial team member for marketing analytics dashboards: IT. You learned the different viewpoints of IT and business managers and how to reconcile them.

In Chapter 6, you got my perspective on establishing the database and measurement system for both in-house and outsourced situations.

Chapter 7 gave you specific tools to generate key performance indicators (KPIs) in structured interviews with stakeholders in your organization.

Chapter 8 tackled the challenging problem of eliminating the wrong KPIs and to discover key leading performance indicators (KLPIs).

Chapter 9 specifically dealt with integrating metrics from traditional and emerging channels, such as online search and social media.

Chapter 10 showed you how differences in emerging and mature markets translate into differences in dashboard metrics and how decision makers can improve them.

Having the right metrics in place, Chapter 11 allows you to design the right structure and visual data display for an effective dashboard prototype.

Chapter 12 provided a checklist for launching the dashboard and overcoming common implementation and renewal challenges.

Chapter 13 showed different ways to act on the dashboard insights: from gradually improving to optimizing the allocation and the size of your marketing budget.

Finally, Chapter 14 dug into the cultural transition in organizations infused with marketing analytics dashboards. The culture and practice of accountability represents a lasting legacy to your organization's DNA.

Sounds long and complicated? This book teaches just four steps: understanding marketing analytics dashboards, planning for them, designing them, and implementing them. Each chapter is driven by my experience across continents and industries of what makes this work in organizations of any size. *And it does work.* In a recent survey of over 200 senior executives, Germann, Lilien, and Rangaswamy[1] uncovered five key success factors for effective use of marketing analytics dashboards that increase company's performance by between 8 and 20 percent:

1. Top management support (see Chapters 1 and 3).

2. A supportive analytics culture (see Chapters 4 and 14).

3. Information technology support (see Chapter 5).

4. Appropriate data (see Chapter 6).

5. Analytic skills (see Chapters 7 through 10 and 13).

Improving any of these areas will help you climb the latter of better marketing insights and decisions. Beyond personal satisfaction, your standing will also increase in the eyes of your colleagues, boss, CEO, or investors

The analytics in this book help you show marketing actions as a justified expense. The dashboard insights help you manage a portfolio of marketing investments. Bringing it all together in a culture of accountability helps you realize the potential as an innovative growth engine for your company.

It is now *up to you* to put this into your practice. Even the best tools fail to produce superior business performance if they are not widely used and incorporated in day-to-day decisions. I'm happy to help, especially in the toughest challenges of (1) identifying the leading indicators that have the largest long-term performance effects and (2) modeling their interactions to enable what-if analyses and predict the impact of different decision options.

Far from extinguishing innovation and creativity, marketing analytics dashboards help marketers take smarter risks by assessing experimental projects and forecasting the profit potential of bigger, bolder initiatives. In marketing as in life, art and science feed off each other.

I wish you the best creative breakthroughs, supported by the best data and analytics to communicate and implement the best insights. Let us move toward this bright future together; share your experiences with me in an email to koen@notthesizeofthedata.com.

Notes

Introduction

1. Berend A. Wierenga and Gerrit H. Van Bruggen, *Marketing Management Support Systems: Principles, Tools, and Implementation* (Vol. 10) (New York: Springer, 2000).
2. Stefan Biesdorf, David Court, and Paul Willmott, "Big Data: What's Your Plan," *McKinsey Quarterly*, March 2013; www.mckinsey.com/insights/business_technology/big_data_whats_your_plan.
3. Frank Germann, Gary L. Lilien, and Arvind Rangaswamy, "Performance Implications of Deploying Marketing Analytics," *International Journal of Research in Marketing*, 30(2), June 2013, 114–128; www.sciencedirect.com/science/article/pii/S0167811612000912.
4. Trip Kucera and David White, "Predictive Analytics for Sales and Marketing: Seeing Around Corners," January 1, 2012, Aberdeen Research group (aberdeen.com/Aberdeen-Library/7082/RA-predictive-business-analytics.aspx) and "McKinsey Global Survey Results: Measuring Marketing," *McKinsey Quarterly*, 2009, 1–8.

Chapter 1

1. John D. C. Little got the first ever PhD in Operations Research (his advisor was a physics professor whose line goes back to Newton) and went on to make many great contributions in management and marketing science. At age eighty-five, his research is fresh as ever; he is currently at the forefront of e-commerce. Key to his work is always a desire to make the complicated understandable, to make the model relevant to managers so that it is used in practice. Who would be better to quote at the start of this book!
2. Germann, Lilien, and Rangaswamy, "Performance Implications."
3. www.youtube.com/watch?v=yfeu4bADkiE.
4. Gail McGovern and Joan A Quelch, "Measuring Marketing Performance," Prod # 507701-MMC-ENG, Feb. 1, 2007.

5. David Reibstein, "Measured Thoughts: Sean Hagerty, CMO, Vanguard," *Marketing NPV*, January 8, 2008; marketingnpv.com/content/measured-thoughts-sean-hagerty-cmo-vanguard.

6. Tim Ambler and John Roberts, "Beware the Silver Metric: Marketing Performance Measurement Has to Be Multidimensional," Marketing Science Institute, Report #06-113 (and rejoinder #06-115), October 2006; www.msi.org/publications/publication.cfm?pub=916.

7. James Lattin and Michael Rierson, "Capital One: Leveraging Information-Based Marketing," 2007: Stanford Graduate School of BusinessProd. #: M316-PDF-EN.

8. Herbert A. Simon, *Models of Man. Social and Rational* (New York, John Wiley and Sons, 1957).

9. Paul Hyde, Edward Landry, and Andrew Tipping, "Making the Perfect Marketer," *Strategy+Business*, Booz Allen Hamilton, 2004.

10. Edward Landry, Andrew Tipping, and Jay Kumar, "Growth Champions," *Strategy+Business*, Booz Allen Hamilton, 2006.

11. Presentation by Avaya at Tuck School of Business at Dartmouth, in "Return on Marketing Investment" MBA elective taught by Koen Pauwels, May 2009.

12. Private conversations with company managers, 2009.

13. Private conversations with company managers, 2009.

14. John Quelch, "William McNabb, Chairman, Vanguard Group." Prod. #: 509731-VIN-ENG; and David Reibstein, "Measured Thoughts: Sean Hagerty."

15. Rick Beatty, "Data Guides, But the Gut Decides," *Ad Age*, February 19, 2013; adage.com/article/cmo-strategy/data-guides-gut-decides/239894/.

Chapter 2

1. Harvey Newman and Cameron Jones, "New Efficiencies Case Study," 2003; fiscal-research.gsu.edu/atlanta_case_study/New%20Efficiences%20Case%20Study.pdf.

2. D. Edwards and J. C. Thomas, "Developing a Municipal Performance–Measurement System: Reflections on the Atlanta Dashboard," *Public Administration Review*, 65(3), 2005, 369–376.

3. Robert S. Kaplan and David P. Norton, "The Balanced Scorecard—Measures That Drive Performance," *Harvard Business Review*, January-February 1992; hbr.org/2005/07/the-balanced-scorecard-measures-that-drive-performance/.

4. Adapted from Newman and Jones, "New Efficiencies."

5. John D. C. Little, "Decision Support Systems for Marketing Managers," *Journal of Marketing*, 1979, 9–26; www.jstor.org/discover/10.2307/1250143?uid=3739832&uid=2&uid=4&uid=3739256&sid=21102622102987.

6. Wikipedia (2013), "Marketing Mix Modeling"; en.wikipedia.org/wiki/Marketing_mix_modeling.

7. Yoram Wind, "Marketing as an Engine of Business Growth: A Cross-Functional Perspective," *Journal of Business Research,* 58, 2005, 863–873.

8. Source: www.marketingpower.com/_layouts/Dictionary.aspx?dLetter=M.

9. Ofer Mintz and Imram S. Currim, "What Drives Managerial Use of Marketing of Marketing and Financial Metrics and Does Metric Use Affect Performance of Marketing-Mix Activities?," *Journal of Marketing,* 77, March 2013, 17–40.

10. Roger J. Best, *Market-Based Management: Strategies for Growing Customer Value and Profitability,* 5th edition (Upper Saddle River, N.J.: Pearson Prentice Hall, 2008), 69.

11. Ibid., 72.

12. Forrester Research, "The Evolved CMO," 2012.

Chapter 3

1. Amy Miller and Jennifer Cioffi, "Measuring Marketing Effectiveness and Value: The Unisys Marketing Dashboard," *Journal of Advertising Research,* September 2004.

2. Bruce H. Clark, Andrew V. Abela, and Tim Ambler, "Behind The Wheel," *Marketing Management,* May/June 2006, 18–36.

3. Roy Young, *Marketing Champions: Practical Strategies for Improving Marketing's Power, Influence, and Business Impact* (New York: Wiley, 2006).

4. Reibstein, "Measured Thoughts: Sean Hagerty."

5. Jeff Zabin, "Follow the Money with Marketing Dashboards," CRM News: E-Marketing, June 2008; www.ecommercetimes.com/story/63252.html.

6. Ibid., p. 3.

7. Ibid., p. 3.

Chapter 4

1. Raymond Young and Ernest Jordan, "Top Management Support: Mantra or Necessity?," *International Journal of Project Management,* 26, 713–725; www.sciencedirect.com/science/article/pii/S0263786308000811.

2. Lynn Crawford et al. (2008), "Governance and Support in the Sponsoring of Projects and Programs," *Project Management Journal,* October 2008, 51.

3. "Actuaries must convince the CEOs of the value of predictive modeling," Casualty Actuarial Society, December 13, 2012; www.casact.org/press/index.cfm?fa=viewArticle&articleID=2125.

Chapter 5

1. Forrester Research, "The Evolved CMO."

2. Biesdorf, Court, and Willmott, "Big Data."

Chapter 6

1. What are URIs? A URI is a persistent, location-independent identifier for resources, which remains globally unique and persistent even when the resource ceases to exist or becomes unavailable. URIs can be classified as locators (URLs), as names (URNs), or as both. A uniform resource name (URN) is like a person's name, while a uniform resource locator (URL) is like that person's street address. In other words, the URN defines an item's identity, while the URL provides a method for finding it. This will help you store references and links to other systems of a firm (contacts databases, sales and operational reporting systems, etc.).

Chapter 7

1. Copyright by BrightPoint Consulting, reprinted with author's permission. For more details, see the website: www.brightpointinc.com/Articles.asp?File=Dashboard%20Design%20Metrics%20and%20KPIs.htm.
2. Tim Ambler, *Marketing and the Bottom Line*, 2nd edition (Upper Saddle River, NJ: Financial Times Prentice Hall, 2003).
3. Koen Pauwels, Jorge Silva-Risso, Shuba Srinivasan, and Dominique M. Hanssens, "New Products, Sales Promotions and Firm Value: The Case of the Automobile Industry," *Journal of Marketing*, 68 (October 2004), 142–156; notthesizeofthedata.com.
4. Ambler, *Marketing and the Bottom Line*.
5. David Reibstein, "Measured Thoughts: Rob Malcolm, CMO, Diageo," Marketing NVP, February 21, 2008; marketingnpv.com/content/measured-thoughts-rob-malcolm-cmo-diageo.

Chapter 8

1. Mintz and Currim, "What Drives Managerial Use of Marketing?"
2. Ambler, *Marketing and the Bottom Line*.
3. James J. Rooney and Lee N. Vanden Heuvel, "Root Cause Analysis for Beginners," *Quality Progress*, 37(7), 2004, 45–56.
4. Martin R. Lautman and Koen Pauwels, "What Is Important? Identifying Metrics That Matter," *Journal of Advertising Research*, 49(3), September 2009, 339–359; notthesizeofthedata.com.
5. Glen L. Urban, "PERCEPTOR: A Model for Product Positioning," *Management Science*, 21, April 1975, 858–871.
6. Koen Pauwels, Selin Erguncu, and Gokhan Yildirim, "Winning Hearts, Minds and Sales: How Marketing Communication Enters the Purchase Process in Emerging and Mature Markets," *International Journal of Research in Marketing* 30(1), 2013, 57–68; notthesizeofthedata.com.

7. Kevin Lane Keller, Brian Sternthal, and Alice M. Tybout, "Three Questions You Need to Ask About Your Brand," *Harvard Business Review*, 80(9), 2002, 80–89.

8. Lautman and Pauwels, "What Is Important?"

9. Dan Marks presentation at Ozyegin University, 2012, and at www.youtube.com/watch?v=91YQc3oDxrA.

10. Clive W. J. Grange, "Investigating Causal Relations by Econometric Methods and Cross-Spectral Methods," *Econometrica*, 37 (1969), 424–438.

11. Christopher A. Sims, "Macroeconomics and Reality," *Econometrica*, 48(1): 1–48.

12. Rebecca Slotegraaf and Koen Pauwels, "The Impact of Brand Equity and Innovation on the Long-Term Effectiveness of Promotions," *Journal of Marketing Research*, 45 (June 2008), 293–306; notthesizeofthedata.com.

13. Grange, "Investigating Causal Relations."

14. For explanatory error, we show (1-R2). For forecasting error, we show the Theil's inequality coefficient.

15. J. Scott Armstrong, *Principles of Forecasting: A Handbook for Researchers and Practitioners* (New York: Springer, 2001).

16. For simulations into an uncertain future, it pays to combine VAR with agent-based models, which can simulate how dynamic interactions among agents (consumers, bloggers, regulators, retailers, etc.) lead to market outcomes. The author has a pending U.S. patent for this combination.

Chapter 9

1. Jonathan Becher, Chief Marketing Officer at SAP; www.forbes.com/sites/sap/2013/02/22/welcome-to-the-future-three-must-dos-for-the-modern-marketer/.

2. Carlota Perez, *Technological Revolutions and Financial Capital: The Dynamics of Bubbles and Golden Ages* (London: Elgar, 2002).

3. The Gartner Group, "Gartner's 2012 Hype Cycle for Emerging Technologies Identifies 'Tipping Point' Technologies That Will Unlock Long-Awaited Technology Scenarios," August 16, 2012; www.gartner.com/newsroom/id/2124315.

4. Jason Del Rey, "Click-Through Rates May Matter Even Less Than We Thought," *Ad Age*, April 24, 2012; adage.com/article/digital/click-rates-matter-thought/234330/.

5. Sunil Gupta, "Solving the Search vs. Display Advertising Quandary," April 15, 2013; hbswk.hbs.edu/faculty/sgupta.html, or notthesizeofthedata.com.

6. Evert de Haan, Thorsten Wiesel, and Koen Pauwels, "Which Advertising Forms Make a Difference in Online Path to Purchase?" *Marketing Science Institute*, Report 13-104, 2013; www.msi.org/reports/which-advertising-forms-make-a-difference-in-online-path-to-purchase/, or notthesizeofthedata.com.

7. Joe Tripodi, *Harvard Business Review*, April 27, 2011; blogs.hbr.org/cs/2011/04/coca-colas_marketing_shift_fro.html.

8. Jeff Molander, "How Avaya Makes Twitter Sell: Successfully Aligning Sales with Marketing," 2012; www.makesocialmediasell.com/twitter-avaya/.

9. Craig Stacey, Koen Pauwels, and Andrew Lackman, "Beyond Likes and Tweets: Measuring the Impact of Social Media," presentation at Measurable Marketing in a Social World Conference, NYU, January 26, 2012; pages.stern.nyu.edu/~atakos/centerresearch/likesandtweetsslidedeck.pdf, or notthesizeofthedata.com.

10. Wendy W. Moe and Michael Trusov, "The Value of Social Dynamics in Online Product Ratings Forums," *Journal of Marketing Research*, 48(3), 2011, 444–456.

11. Stacey, Pauwels, Lackman, "Beyond Likes and Tweets," 2012.

12. D. Godes et al., "Firm's Management of Social Interactions," *Marketing Letters* 16(3/4), 2005, 415–428.

13. Marketing Center Muenster and Roland Berger Strategy Consultants, "Social Media Think:Lab Thought Leaders' Summit 2012"; www.socialmediathinklab.com/science-summit-2012/.

Chapter 10

1. Theodore Levitt, "The Globalization of Markets," *Harvard Business Review*, 61(2), May 1983, 92–102; hbr.org/1983/05/the-globalization-of-markets.

2. Jan-Benedict E. M. Steenkamp and Inge Geyskens, "Manufacturer and Retailer Strategies to Impact Store Brand Share: Global Integration, Local Adaptation and Worldwide Learning," *Europanel GIE Presentation*, 2012; www.europanel.com/files/Feature1207PLstrategies.pdf.

3. Ming-Jer Chen, *Inside Chinese Business: A Guide for Managers Worldwide* (Boston: Harvard Business School Press, 2001).

4. Kuntara Pukthuanthong and Richard Roll, "Global Market Integration: An Alternative Measure and Its Application," *Journal of Financial Economics*, 94, 2009, 214–232.

5. Elihu Katz and Paul Lazarsfeld, *Personal Influence: The Part Played by People in the Flow of Mass Communications* (New York: The Free Press, 1955).

6. Nielsen Media Research, "Nielsen Global Online Consumer Survey – Trust, Value, and Engagement in Advertising"; hk.acnielsen.com/documents/NielsenTrustAdvertisingGlobalReportJuly09.pdf

7. Stephen Michael Burgess and Jan-Benedict E. M. Steenkamp, "Marketing Renaissance: How Research in Emerging Markets Advances Marketing Science and Practice," *International Journal of Research in Marketing*, 23, 2006, 337–356; www.sciencedirect.com/science/article/pii/S0167811606000607.

8. Pauwels, Erguncu, and Yildirim, "Winning Hearts, Minds and Sales."

9. Wei-Shien Wang, "How Culture Influences the Brand Association in the United Kingdom and Taiwan: A Case Study of L'Oreal Paris," Master's thesis, 2006, University of Central Florida.
10. G. Thomas M. Hult et al., "Organizational Learning in Global Supply Management: A Model and Test of Internal Users and Corporate Buyers," *Decision Sciences*, 31(2), 2000, 293–325.
11. Based on Pauwels, Erguncu, and Yildrim, "Winning Hearts, Minds and Sales."
12. Julie Halpert, "Hyundai Marketing Boss: We're Not Just a 'Left-Brain Choice,'" Oct. 10, 2011; adage.com/article/news/hyundai-marketing-boss-a-left-brain-choice/230305/.

Chapter 11

1. Jennifer Veesenmeyer; www.youtube.com/watch?v=qR8SU_Bf1wY.
2. PureShare Whitepaper, "Metrics Dashboard Design: Designing Effective Metrics Management Dashboards"; www.pureshare.com/resources/resource_files/pureshare_dashboard_design.pdf.
3. Tom Davenport in his April 4, 2013, Harvard Business Review blog; blogs.hbr.org/cs/2013/04/how_p_and_g_presents_data.html.
4. Ibid.
5. Ibid.

Chapter 12

1. Daryl Orts, "Dashboard Implementation Methodology," *DM Review*, June 2005; www.information-management.com/issues/20050601/1028733-1.html.
2. Brian Ballou, Dan L. Heitger, and Laura Donnell, "Creating Effective Dashboards: How Companies Can Improve Executive Decision-Making and Board Oversight," *Strategic Finance*, March 2010, 28–32; www.imanet.org/PDFs/Public/SF/2010_03/03_2010_ballou.pdf.
3. Nelson, "Critical Dashboard Project Success Factors That Most Tend to Miss," Datavism, April 28, 2011; datavism.com/blog/critical-dashboard-project-success-factors-that-most-tend-to-miss/.

Chapter 13

1. www.smartbrief.com/08/18/09/there-are-two-ways-get-fired-harrahs-stealing-company-or-failing-include-proper-control#.UjLhosbddO0.
2. De Haan, Wiesel, and Pauwels, "Which Advertising Forms Make a Difference?"
3. Joep Arts, Thorsten Wiesel, and Koen Pauwels, "Practice-Prize Paper: Marketing's Profit Impact: Quantifying Online and Offline Funnel Progression," *Marketing Science*, 30(4), 2011, 604–611; notthesizeofthedata.com.

4. Robert Dorfman and Peter O. Steiner, "Optimal Advertising and Optimal Quality," *American Economic Review*, 44(5), December 1954, 826–836; www.jstor.org/discover/10.2307/1807704?uid=3739832&uid=2&uid=4&uid=3739256&sid=21102654641307.

5. Malcolm Wright, "A New Theorem for Optimizing the Advertising Budget," *Journal of Advertising Research*, 49(2), June 2009, 164–169.

6. Peter J. Danaher, André Bonfrer, and Sanjay Dhar. "The Effect of Competitive Advertising Interference on Sales for Packaged Goods," *Journal of Marketing Research*, 45.2, 2008, 211–225.

7. Shuba Srinivasan, Koen Pauwels, Jorge Silva-Risso, and Dominique M. Hanssen, "Product Innovations, Marketing Investments and Stock Returns," *Journal of Marketing*, 73(1), January 7, 2009, 24–43.

8. Martin Natter, Thomas Reutterer, Andreas Mild, and Alfred Taudes, "An Assortmentwide Decision-Support System for Dynamic Pricing and Promotion Planning in DIY Retailing," *Marketing Science*, 26(4), 2007, 576–583.

9. Ibid.

10. Gary L. Lilien, John H. Roberts, and Venkatesh Shankar, "Effective Marketing Science Applications: Insights from ISMS-MSI Practice Prize Finalist Papers and Projects," *Marketing Science*, 32(2), March–April 2013, 229–245.

11. Ibid.

12. Ibid.

13. Fred D. Davis, Richard P. Bagozzi, and Paul R Warshaw, "User Acceptance of Computer Technology: A Comparison of Two Theoretical Models," *Management Science*, 35(8), August 1989, 982–1003; and George J. Avlonitis and Nikolaos G. Panagopoulos, "Antecedents and Consequences of CRM Technology Acceptance in the Sales Force," *Industrial Marketing Management*, 34(4), May 2005, 355–368.

Chapter 14

1. Germann, Lilien, and Rangaswamy, "Performance Implications."

2. Colin Dover, "How Dashboards Can Change Your Culture," *Strategic Finance*, 86(4), October 2004, 43–48; www.thefreelibrary.com/How+dashboards+can+change+your+culture%3A+companies+become...-a0123085925.

3. McGovern and Quelch, "Measuring Marketing Performance."

4. David Rogers and Don Sexton, "Marketing ROI in the Era of Big Data," 2012; www.iab.net/media/file/2012-BRITE-NYAMA-Marketing-ROI-Study.pdf.

Conclusion

1. Germann, Lilien, and Rangaswamy, "Performance Implications."

Index

About the Author

PROFESSOR KOEN PAUWELS integrates research, teaching, and consultancy across Asia, America, and Europe. He is the most published and awarded researcher on marketing performance, with more than thirty peer reviewed publications and over 3,000 citations. He won the 2010 *Google/WPP Research Award*, the 2011 *Syntec* (Association of French Consultants) Best Paper in Marketing/Decision Sciences Award, the 2001 *EMAC* best paper award, the 2007 O'Dell award for the most influential paper in the *Journal of Marketing Research*, the 2008 and 2009 *Emerald* Management Reviews Citation of Excellence, the 2009 and 2011 Davidson awards for the best paper in *Journal of Retailing*, and the 2009 Varadarajan Award for *Early Career Contributions* to *Marketing Strategy Research. Pauwels* was chosen as a Top 100 Highly Inspirational Alumnus out of 37,000 UCLA Anderson School alumni. His academic publications appear in four text books and other publications such as *Harvard Business Review, Adweek,* the *GfK Marketing Intelligence Review,* and the Marketing Science Institute reports.

Professor Pauwels has taught in executive education at UCLA, the Tuck School of Business at Dartmouth, Cannes Golden Lions, Geneva (HEC), Mainz (GfK Academy), Manisa (Turkey), and Jaipur (India). He is the first expert in Research/Metrics on the discussion forum at Marketingprofs.com, a global community of over half a million busi -ness professionals.

Pauwels is the cofounder of the Marketing Productivity Group (USA) and the digital marketing coordinator at AIMark (Europe). He has consulted for dozens of companies including Heinz, Kayak.com, Marks & Spencer, Nissan, Sony Eurasia, Tetrapak and Unilever. His work at medium-sized company Inofec generated a 14-fold increase in profit in the field experiment that implemented his advice; he was a finalist for the prestigious Marketing Science Practice Prize for that work.

Pauwels was born in Belgium in 1971 and became a commercial engineer before moving to the United States, where he graduated with a PhD in Management at UCLA in 2001. Next he climbed the academic ladder at the Tuck School of Business at Dartmouth and got tenure in 2005. Joining the startup Ozyegin University in 2008, he moved to Istanbul, where he lives with his wife and their two boys.